A Word from the Publisher

Mission Nation Publishing was begun to give a voice to missionaries the Lord is sending to America today. One of these is Dr. Shang Ik Moon, known to everyone as Professor Moon. Few people have come into the world so far from God and have suffered so much as Professor Moon. He grew up as a child in what is now North Korea during World War II. At the end of the war, as a twelve-year-old boy, he endured a painful and hazardous escape from the North to South Korea just before the Korean War began.

His family was decimated in that war, and young Shang Ik was reduced to finding shelter on the ground under an improvised tent and food in garbage dumps.

Mission Nation Publishing was begun to give a voice to the missionaries to America. That seems strange to our ears. A missionary to America? Why? America sends missionaries to other countries. But there has been a steady decline of Christianity in the United States.

But the Lord is calling missionaries to America to strengthen the church.

Too many times these women and men are treated like second-class citizens. Yet many have stories to tell, tales of great faith and incredible courage. The stories give courage to those on the front lines of the mission field in America. The accounts demonstrate that these missionaries are gifts given to us by a loving God.

You can see over forty video interviews, read my blog about the missionaries, and find resources for reaching out to immigrants on the Mission Nation Publishing website, www.MissionNationPublishing.org. Go to the website, listen to the missionaries, and please keep them and Mission Nation Publishing in your prayers.

Robert Scudieri
President and Publisher
December 4, 2017

Contents

Notes to Korean Words

Halmeoni (grandmother)
Appa (father)
Eomma (mother)
Uibus-Eomi (stepmother)
Eomeonim (mother-in-law)
Jageun Appa   (father's younger brother)
Jageun-Eomma (the wife of your father's younger brother)
Azumma (lady, a woman of respect)
Won (South Korean currency)

It has been proven to me personally that death is indeed very imminent, always around us, but if we have any breath at all at any given time, it is because God still intervenes in our lives, and the ultimate example of that is the life and death of Jesus Christ and the resulting redemptive work and our eternal home.

—Shang Ik Moon

Mission Nation Publishing published this book with the support of the following:

Senior Publishers

John and Linda Friend
Concordia University Irvine

Publishers

Professor Kou Seying
Professor Andrew Bartelt
Anonymous
Jane Aller
Ben and Cecilia Haupt
Jim Schlie
Dr. Yared Halche
Robert and Lynn Scudieri

Prologue

South Korea,1951. The cherry blossom trees withered with the cold. Their twisted branches lined the streets in the village of Uh-Jung-Geh, creating an eerie border. The town was situated twenty miles south of the city of Seoul. Snow rested gently on top of thatched roofs over small mud huts. The mountainous backdrop of the village was the picture of serenity. Most of the people had fled south to avoid the encroaching North Korean army.

A lone swallow sang its morning song as it flittered from empty branch to empty branch. After a moment, a young woman refugee exited a straw-thatched farmhouse, straw basket in hand. Fleeing the danger in Seoul, she and her family had found shelter in the abandoned village. She made her way toward the outskirts of the small town, traveling down a hidden pathway bordered by persimmon trees.

The valley was serene as the young woman carried her basket of clothing toward the stream to wash. She paused at the sound of her little son's laughter in the small hut. Chuckling and shaking her head, she turned and continued walking. She could imagine him getting into some sort of mischief while her younger brother tried to corral the energetic little boy. She pictured him running wild in his bare feet while her baby daughter slept unfazed in her tiny bassinet.

The sounds of her children and brother faded gently into the wind with the swallow's song as she approached a stream they used for washing and bathing. The young woman set down her basket, tucking her long, jet-black hair into a plain brown headscarf. She reached into the basket she had set on the smooth river stones, carefully removing one item of clothing after another. Beginning first with her baby's soft cream-colored nightdress, she submerged it into the frigid water. She entered a rhythmic pattern of scrubbing the clothing on the smooth river rocks, dunking one article at a time into the water, wringing dry, scrubbing and pounding again, dunking, and then wringing dry one last time.

She worked quickly, periodically stopping to blow warm breath on her hands and shake off the winter cold. So focused was she on her task that the cadence of her pounding and wringing and the splashing of the water as she dunked and scrubbed drowned out the humming sound at first.

But when she stopped to drape a nightshirt onto the charcoal gray rocks to dry, she heard it—a distant yet distinct buzzing sound. She was about to shrug it off and return to her laundry when the sound became louder, pulling her away from the water. She drew her hands to her eyes and turned her face toward the sky as she slowly stood to her feet. With her hands shielding her eyes from the vibrant rays of the sun, she made a squinted attempt to distinguish the image on the horizon. The figure in the sky took shape, drawing all color from her ruddy cheeks and creating a hallowed gasp from lips that no longer shivered with the cold.

In the air, the fighter plane descended onto the valley at breakneck speed. The young pilot craned his neck from inside the cockpit of his B-26 Invader. He tried to clean the foggy window with his gloved hand as he peered and squinted at the ground below. Grunting, he tipped his wings from left to right, trying to get a better angle of the figure at the water. All he saw from above was violent thrusting movements on the water's edge.

His heart raced. He knew he had to make a decision quickly. *Why are they digging into the ground? What if they are trying to bury weapons? Or a bomb?*

Pursing his lips, he shook his head, unsure. At the sight of the wings tipping from left to right as the aircraft made a clear descent, the young mother abandoned her wash and turned with a desperate sprint toward the village, where her children were.

The pilot watched as the figure below began to run. The pilot tightened his grip on the yoke of the aircraft and then lifted his radio using his call sign to signal his commander.

"I have a possible tally making a beeline toward the village. How should I proceed?"

He heard a few moments of static on the other end as the plane hovered ominously behind the woman while the pilot waited for confirmation on how to proceed. The radio crackled to life after a moment with a single phrase. "You are clear to engage."

The pilot took a deep breath and then positioned his aircraft directly behind the fleeing figure. He moved his hand off the radio and onto the lever that lowered the high-powered machine gun from the nozzle of the plane.

By this time, the young woman was in hysterics, waving her hands and screaming like a banshee. The deafening sound of the engine of the B-26 drowned out her terrified plea. The boom of the machine gun was more like cannon fire as the bullets chased the woman into the town.

They found their target in the courtyard just outside the small mud and straw cottage. Plants, shrubbery, soil, and chips of wood and stone exploded into the air. The children inside the home dropped to the ground. The walls were instantly shredded, and sharp glass covered every surface. There were screams of despair, and then there was silence.

The hum of the aircraft faded into the distance, taking with it all hope of life as those who survived kept their faces to the ground, terrified of what they would find when they raised their heads.

A Boy Alone

Five Years Earlier

An explosive ten-year-old boy raced down the dirt road in a remote, peaceful village near Heung-Nam, in the Northern region of Korea. Shang Ik Moon panted as he ran with the enthusiasm only an adolescent boy could muster. His side hurt from running so hard, but he grinned, not caring. He was red-faced and sweating. His arms and legs pumped as if he were fleeing dragons. He jumped deftly over a small brook and entered the village like a bullet, kicking up dust and disturbing the beloved chickens of his neighbor, Mrs. Yuri, in the process.

Rushing past a line of small cottages with thatched roofs, he maintained his speed until he reached his *halmeoni*'s home. Using his hands to brake himself against the house, he paused to catch his breath outside the window. After he slowed his breathing to a somewhat normal pace, he peeked inside and smiled. He was here.

In the modest seating area of the home sat his father. Chun-Soo sat comfortably on a chair, sipping tea with Shang Ik's *halmeoni*, nodding his head as she chatted with him. Shang Ik moved closer to the window, standing on his tiptoes so he could see more clearly. The man inside was of humble stature, but he had a commanding presence.

Chun-Soo chuckled lightly into his teacup at the sight of a tiny dark head of hair peering at him from the outside. He didn't interrupt his conversation with his elderly mother, but he did lock eyes with the boy, smiling as he continued sipping his tea. Shang Ik held his father's gaze, still breathing heavily, this time with nervous anticipation.

Chun-Soo slowly lowered his teacup and cleared his throat. "Would you excuse me,

Eomma? I think I'd like to take a walk outside."

Shang Ik propelled himself away from the window and ran toward the back of the cottage just as his father exited the front door. Chun-Soo whistled jovially with his hands in his pockets. He looked up at the sky as if observing the weather. Calmly he removed a gold pocket watch from his pocket and stared down at it, tapping it absentmindedly. Returning it to his pocket, he took a step or two away from the front door.

His feet barely touched the dust on that second step when seventy pounds of adolescence violently toppled him to the ground. Shang Ik manfully tried to maintain his hold on his father, but Chun-Soo playfully bested all his attempts, laughing with glee at his son's red-faced efforts to slip away from his grasp. Father and son had a few more moments of playful wrestling before they settled down, eventually landing on the bottom step of the simple mud and straw home.

Shang Ik could not sit still on the step as he chirped energetically like an eager chipmunk, leaning against his father and then jumping up and down excitedly while he told him about his day and his friends at school. His small hands were a blur in front of his face as he gestured and emphasized wildly. The boy would hop onto the dirt and mimic something funny he had seen or heard, but he always returned quickly to the step, making sure to leave as little space between them as possible.

For his part, Chun-Soo was mostly silent. He smiled at Shang Ik, resting his chin in his hands as he watched his son's animated dialogue before him. He was grateful at least that the boy seemed happy. He appeared to be enjoying school and had plenty of good friendships to keep him company. He always worried, among other things, for instance, that his boy would be too lonely in this little cottage with only an old woman and some neighborhood chickens for company.

Shang Ik could not contain his excitement whenever his father came to visit. His father was his best friend. There was no one more important in Shang Ik's little world than his father. He had recently remarried, but Shang Ik had not been able to attend the wedding. His new *uibus-eomi* seemed nice enough in her letters to Shang Ik. She sent presents and promised she was looking forward to meeting him and having them live together as a family. Shang Ik desperately hoped that was true, if only because he knew it meant his time away from his father would really be over.

Whenever his father did come to see him, Shang Ik felt like he was making up for lost time. His nervous energy culminated on the final day of his father's visits into a plea, the same appeal he always made, to be taken with him.

For his part, Chun-Soo was silent as his son rattled on about his childish affairs. Chun-Soo pretended to listen as best as he could, but his mind was on other things, among them his work, his responsibilities, and his regret.

During the Japanese occupation of Korea from 1910 to the end of World War II in 1945, as a young man, he had left his village to go to Japan to be educated as a lawyer. He left his young wife and baby, Shang Ik, with his mother while he continued his studies.

Shang Ik had learned of his mother's death from a fatal illness at an early age. He still remembers the day his *halmeoni* told him. The village children would often play together during the day, and for a while, he had noticed they would run home when their mothers came calling. Often a mother would come out to scold a child or to bring him or her home by the ear.

It was then that he asked his grandmother as they puttered around her small garden. Where was his *eomma*? Didn't he have one? From that moment on, *Halmeoni* told the story of her illness and how important it was for his father to be in Japan working and studying to give Shang Ik a better life.

She repeated the story for him, as if to make sure he didn't forget. That was years ago. He hadn't forgotten, but he did spend many nights trying to make sense of his feelings as he lay on his small cot. Why did he miss her? He felt sad in a way he couldn't understand.

When his father remarried and sent word to Shang Ik, he should have felt happy. He finally had a mother. She seemed nice enough from her letters and expressed eagerness for the time when Shang Ik could finally live with them. Shang Ik would smile as his *halmeoni* read the letters and nodded his head when she said, "Isn't this wonderful, Shang Ik? One day you will live with your father and new mother, and you will be a very happy boy."

He enthusiastically agreed and skipped out of the house to play. But that night as he lay in bed, the feelings returned. He was barely secure that he had his father. What excitement could he feel about having a new mother? He would clench his fist under his chin as he lay in bed, trying to feel ease with a situation that caused him daily anxiety and tension.

It did not help that after his father became a lawyer he remained in Seoul because the Japanese had established a provincial government of occupation there. His father worked for that government, using his newly acquired law degree to facilitate the relationship between the Japanese and his Korean compatriots.

For years, Chun-Soo insisted that Shang Ik remain in the North with his *halmeoni* and his aunts and uncles. There he would be safe, especially from those who might retaliate against a lawyer who had collaborated with the Japanese occupation.

Japanese imperialism had attempted to eradicate Korean culture while it tried to integrate Korea into the Empire of Japan. Shang Ik was left in the Northern part of Korea with his family, but still the boy learned to speak fluent Japanese since his school had not allowed him to speak Korean.

Recently, though, American and Soviet armies had captured the peninsula, ending the Japanese rule over Korea. This might have been a cause for celebration for some, but for Shang Ik's father, it was the catalyst for much turmoil. How would the victorious allies treat a collaborator?

Japanese occupation of the Korean Peninsula had been handled through the general government, where Shang Ik's father worked. But now the Japanese had surrendered to Allied forces, ending the Second World War. Korea was returning to self-governance for the first time in thirty years. But there was another complication: Korea was now under two separate systems of government, the North backed by the USSR and the South backed by the United States, separated by the 38th parallel as part of war settlements decided at the Potsdam conference in July 1945.

This current state of affairs was a cause of immense family strain because Shang Ik's father, at least for now, had found a job working for the Southern government of Korea while his child was trapped under the influence of the Northern government. He wanted desperately to reunite his family, but given the current political climate and the uncertainty of the future of the two governments, he felt it best to leave Shang Ik in the North with his *halmeoni* until it was safe for them to be together.

This decision was a logical one, determined through much consideration of practical reality. But what was logic to a child? Through the years, Shang Ik had become an anxious, needy, skittish ball of energy. His normal growth seemed hampered by the undue pressures of not knowing when his father would return, if he could ever. And the emotional burden of separation on a child has lasting effects. What does it mean if your father is OK to live without you? To remarry and move on with his life without you? Was he slowly being forgotten?

Shang Ik did not fully comprehend the reality of the desperate attempts Chun-Soo had taken to come to the North as often as he did to see his boy. The last few times, he had to sneak across the border. Both the North and the South were clamoring to claim control over Korea, and until he knew which way that argument would go, endangering Shang Ik's life was not a risk Chun-Soo was willing to take.

And so the boy remained in the North and his father would return to the South, the two separated by nervous anxiety and tense apprehension. But when they were together, there was no danger. There was no war. Nothing was unknown. There was only the two of them and their love for each other. There was just their palpable bond and the underlying reality that all they really wanted out of this life was each other.

Now on the steps of their humble ancestral home, Shang Ik wasted no time chatting away in the twilight. He desperately attempted to squeeze months of information into the few days they had together. For his part, Chun-Soo struggled to suppress his feelings of frustration and fear in order to be fully present for his young son. Once it was obvious that Shang Ik had no more stories to share, the man hugged his little boy close. The boy clung to his father, breathing in his smell and his love. Too soon it was time to go in and prepare for bed.

Both took a drink of water from the pump outside. Chun-Soo took a rag and washed the sweat and dirt off Shang Ik's face and body. Inside, Shang Ik allowed his father to help him into a change of clothes, something he always rebuffed from his *halmeoni* whenever she tried. The boy nestled into his small bed as his father sat on the floor next to him.

"*Appa?*"

Chun-Soo sighed. He knew what was coming. "Yes, Shang Ik?"

"Couldn't I go back with you this time? I promise I will be very careful and obedient to you. I've been very good here, and I won't be any trouble for you or my new *uibis-eomi.*"

"My son…"

"My teacher says I speak the best Japanese in the whole class, and I even speak it better than *Halmeoni*. I could go to work with you if you want!"

"Shang Ik, slow down."

The boy sat up energetically, desperate to present his case. "I could go to school and help you with your work, and we could just be together!"

"Stop it, Shang Ik."

Shang Ik caught his breath as his shoulders slumped. He quietly lay his head back onto the pillow, knowing the answer. Chun-Soo sighed again, not of frustration but of weakness. He would do just about anything to bring his son with him to the South. He would much rather they be together than separated by two different governments.

But each journey across that 38th parallel to visit Shang Ik came with risks to his life. The North and South were growing increasingly hostile toward each other. This wasn't the time to take careless risks. He would endanger his life to see his son, but he would not endanger his child's.

Chun-Soo looked down at his hands for a moment and then up at the boy, and he smiled with compassion. "My son, don't worry so much. I'm sure this business between the North and the South will work itself out very soon. We will all be together before you know it."

Shang Ik simply lowered his eyes. His mouth formed into a pout.

"However, until that happens, we all have to make sacrifices, don't we? I must continue my work in the South, and you have to stay here with *Halmeoni*. You're helping me out a lot right now by being a good boy and a big help to her. You will continue doing that, can't you?"

Shang Ik narrowed his eyes, nodded his head, and pulled the sheet up to his chin. Under the covers, he turned his back to his father. The man stayed kneeling on the floor for a few minutes longer, watching his son. Shang Ik kept his head buried under the blanket until his father gently patted his back and walked out of the room. Hot tears stung the little boy's eyes and dampened his mattress.

A few days later, Shang Ik stood at the small wooden gate that marked the entrance to his *halmeoni*'s village. Chun-Soo was hugging his mother goodbye as she sent him off with wishes of good fortune for his journey, her soft eyes wet with tears. Shang Ik leaned against the gate with his head down until his *halmeoni* finally released his father from the viselike grip of her wrinkled hands. Chun-Soo took a deep breath and knelt before his little boy. He placed both hands on Shang Ik's shoulders, playfully shaking him, trying to get him to smile.

Usually Shang Ik would break into a giggle by the first shake of his shoulder, but today he kept his eyes to the ground, mostly to stop himself from crying. He was at the age where he didn't want his father to see him cry.

Chun-Soo stopped shaking him and pursed his lips, peering at him intently. When Shang Ik refused to look him in the eye, he lowered his head and then brought the boy into his arms for an embrace.

He rested his face on his son's dark hair. Then he separated himself and wearily marched out of the village, down the road toward Heung-Nam. He would stop there to purchase supplies for his journey across the 38th parallel. Shang Ik watched as his father walked away and then turned and ran past his *halmeoni* to the house, rubbing the tears out of his eyes as he ran. His father rounded the corner and continued walking, not bothering to wipe the tears out of his own eyes.

Shang Ik Takes a Stand

Shang Ik tried his best to return to his routine after his father left. His disappointment with this trip felt more burdensome than in times past. Perhaps because he was growing and thought that his father might see him as a young man and not as a little boy. He spent more time than usual in a dark cloud that his *halmeoni* could not shake him from, no matter how hard she tried.

Halmeoni needed his help more and more these days, and Shang Ik welcomed the extra chores to distract him from wallowing over his father. *Halmeoni* relied heavily on Shang Ik, and he gladly made use of his energy by hoeing the little garden, running to the market or his uncle's village, washing clothes, pulling weeds, or gathering firewood. In the late afternoons when he returned from school, he quietly picked up his rake or a bucket and commenced whatever task she had left for him to complete.

Such was their routine that Shang Ik did not think it odd when *Halmeoni* stayed sleeping one morning after the rooster crowed and he got up to get ready for school. She slept a lot more these days, so Shang Ik knew not to disturb her. He simply laid firewood in the kitchen for when she needed it later and set out her coffee.

Mrs. Yuri had dropped off eggs for them already that morning, so Shang Ik knew he would have to feed her chickens when he returned from school, as was their agreement.

After he got ready and ate an apple with a slice of bread, he grabbed his schoolbooks and ran out the door, shouting over his shoulder as he left, "Goodbye, *Halmeoni*!"

He stopped at the pump quickly to pour some cold water over his face and to take a drink.

He didn't bother to dry his face as he ran out of the village, and Mrs. Yuri's chickens angrily fluttered and scuttled out of his path. He resisted the boyish urge to kick one and send it flying, having the presence of mind to note that Mrs. Yuri would no longer be willing to share her eggs with them if he indulged that temptation.

At school, he forced himself to enjoy the day with his friends and teacher instead of thinking about his father, Japan, and the 38th parallel. His Japanese lesson received his usual high marks, and he shrugged his shoulders sheepishly as his teacher commended his work.

After some vigorous play with his schoolmates and another test in the afternoon, Shang Ik gathered his things for the walk home. Skipping through woods and small dirt roads, he swung his books in his arms, wanting to prolong the ordeal of interacting with those ornery chickens as long as possible.

When he first entered the village, he hadn't noticed the crowd. He had been trying to sneak past Mrs. Yuri's and was so focused on that task that the unusual sight of a crowd of people around the doorway of his grandmother's house escaped him. When he turned from Mrs. Yuri's with a satisfied smirk, he stopped short. His grandmother's small cottage home was teeming with people. He recognized some neighbors standing idly by outside, and he thought he heard his uncle's voice coming through the multitude.

Shang Ik shoved his way past the people, pushing through arms and legs until he found himself in the kitchen. He dropped his arms, and his books slipped from his grasp onto the floor with a bang, catching the attention of the adults in the room.

His uncle, his father's younger brother, noticed and stood up from the table, coming over to kneel in front of the boy. He paused before him and then placed his hands on his nephew's shoulders to steady him. It was then that Shang Ik exhaled, not realizing he had been holding his breath since he walked into the home.

"Shang Ik, today your *halmeoni* became very sick. While you were at school, Mrs. Yuri came to call on her, and...well..." His uncle looked up at his wife, unsure of how to proceed.

She came and knelt next to her husband. Taking hold of his limp hand, she caressed the child's face and tried to console him. "Shang Ik, *Halmeoni* was having trouble breathing, and her heart stopped. She's passed on. She was very old, and she just became too weak. She's gone now. Do you understand, child?"

Shang Ik simply stared at his aunt's face, completely unsure of what he should say or do. His relatives' faces were full of pity and gentleness, but all Shang Ik could really notice was the fact that it wasn't his father's face.

His aunt addressed him once more. "Shang Ik, do you understand?"

He nodded. "Yes, *Jageun-Eomma.*"

His uncle put his hand on the boy's shoulder. "You go with your aunt while I talk to the doctor, OK, Shang Ik?"

Shang Ik's entire body slumped as he allowed his aunt to lead him toward the small table in the seating area. There was no formal kitchen or living room, so one of the older relatives stood from the small sofa to allow the boy to sit.

Shang Ik's aunt took the boy's hand. "Sit here, Shang Ik. I'll give you some warm tea. Sounds good, hmm?" She gently patted his hand and turned to pour the tea.

From his place on the sofa, he could see into *Halmeoni*'s bedroom. His tiny grandmother lay on the bed, quiet and peaceful. *Maybe they made a mistake. She's just sleeping. She must still be sleeping.*

The people moved around him with a quiet hum as he stared into the bedroom. He noticed Dr. Hwan in the room, moving from the bed to the small table and placing items into his medical bag. The doctor and his uncle stood speaking for a few moments while Shang Ik watched them. The doctor shook his head at his uncle and then walked over and adjusted some blankets by the foot of the bed. Moving to stand directly over *Halmeoni*'s body, he looked at his pocket watch, sighed, and covered her face with the blanket.

As the blanket settled over *Halmeoni*'s serene face, Shang Ik's small fist involuntarily flew to his chest as his heart began to beat uncontrollably and his breathing grew shallow. Suddenly the people and shapes in the room melded together in one haze of undetectable color and sound. Shang Ik shifted to the edge of the seat and clutched tighter at his chest. His shoulders heaved up and down as he tried to get some air into his lungs.

He heard his aunt's voice through the noise, sounding almost muffled and in slow motion. "Do you still like four sugar cubes in your tea, Shang Ik? Shang Ik?"

Shang Ik threw himself off the sofa and pushed aside the people and objects in his way. Bolting from the home at top speed, he violently pushed past the crowd, fleeing from the sound of his uncle and aunt calling his name as tears flowed freely from his eyes.

Shang Ik kept running, this time not caring how many chickens he kicked as he bolted from the village and toward the wooded area that bordered the main road. He ran headfirst into the foliage until his uncle's call was faint in the distance. The evening air brought a nighttime medley from the animals as Shang Ik stumbled through the forest, still clutching at his chest. The foliage grew thicker and more congested the further in he ran until his foot hit an above-ground root and he fell firmly onto his knees.

He stayed there with his palms in the cool dirt beneath him as tears dropped onto the leaves. He took labored breaths until his tears subsided. Wiping his face with the back of his hand, he looked up into the sky. The stars were hidden behind the leaves of the trees, and in that dark cocoon of wilderness, the little ten-year-old boy was overwhelmed with how small and alone he felt.

As he sat on his knees, his labored breathing ringing in his ears, one thought rang through the parade of fear in his mind. *What will Appa say?*

Shang Ik sat there as images of his *halmeoni* flooded his mind—*Halmeoni* singing songs with him as they worked in her garden, *Halmeoni* cooking him his favorite meal, *Halmeoni* rubbing his back when he wasn't feeling well, and *Halmeoni* making the long walk to the schoolroom when his teacher wanted to speak to the parents.

Halmeoni, his *halmeoni*. She was his mother, his father, and his friend. And now she was gone. And he wouldn't be able to tell her how much he loved her and how sorry he was that he had ever been a burden. *I'm alone. I will be all alone. What if Appa can never come for me now? What if he never wanted to?*

Hours passed as he sat with his knees in the mud and his palms in the dirt. The darkness settled around him, shielding him as if it knew he needed time alone.

Eventually he raised his head and rolled his neck. He stood from the ground, more dirty and tired than a day of playing had ever made him. As he trudged home through the thicket, stumbling to find his way in the dark, he began to worry about the repercussions he would receive for running away. He also did not want to have to face the question of what would become of him. He did not want to have to wake up the next morning, not knowing if he would ever see his *appa* again.

Eventually he found a clearing in the woods and was able to find the main road. He entered the village gate and noticed that the crowd of people had gone from *Halmeoni*'s house. Only a small lamp was shining in the window of the little cottage. He walked slowly up to the home, taking each step at a snail's pace. Once he reached the top step, he could hear snippets of the conversation going on inside. Crouching down, he snuck over to the window to listen.

"It's getting late. Don't you think one of us should go look for him now?"

"I told you. The boy just became frightened. It's hard for him with Chun-Soo not here."

"Yes, that's true. He'll come back soon enough, and then we can decide what to do."

There was a pause as teacups clanged with saucers and small spoons stirred hot liquid. Shang Ik pressed his ear as close as he could to the window, wanting to catch every word.

He heard his uncle's anxious voice. "I still think it is best that he stays with me. My children are grown. I can give him more time. The child needs that."

This did not sit well with his aunt. "But, Brother, you live so far from Heung-Nam. I think it best that he stays close by, where he can go to the same school and have the same friends. That is what he needs right now. That's why he should stay with me."

"Oh, how can you suggest that? You have three small children of your own. Where would you get the energy?"

Just then the wooden door swung open and slammed into the wall, interrupting their discussion. In the doorway stood a slightly dirty, red-faced, but otherwise unharmed Shang Ik. Before they could react to his stony presence or his disheveled appearance, the boy opened his mouth with a determined exclamation.

"I want to go with *Appa*."

Shang Ik's uncle shook himself out of his reverie and jumped up, grabbing the boy by the shoulders and wagging his finger at him. "Where have you been? What do you mean worrying the family like that? How dare you just take off in that way without telling us and staying out as late as you did?"

Shang Ik tried to squirm out of his uncle's firm grasp. "I'm sorry, *Jageun Appa.*"

His aunt stood from her chair and came to him, scolding more gently. "Shang Ik, we were very worried. You have had no dinner. Come sit down and eat something before you go to bed."

She began to pull on the boy's arm, but he resisted. "No, *Jageun-Eomma.* Wait. I…"

Another uncle stood up with enthusiasm. "Well, Shang Ik, since you are back, how would you like to come stay with me at my home? Come, boy. You will have a nice time with us on the farm."

Shang Ik snatched his arm away from his aunt's grasp and pulled away from his uncle's firm hands. "No!"

The others stopped chatting and maneuvering, shocked at his outburst. There he stood, small but steady in the doorway. He set his face with determination and squared his shoulders to show his seriousness. Satisfied he had their attention, he made his wishes as clear as possible: only one option would be met with his absolute approval.

"I want to go with *Appa*. I am sorry, *Jageun Appa*. I am sorry I have worried you all and ran off without a word. I will never do so again. But please, I want to go with my *appa*. Please tell him to come for me."

His uncle began to pace, rubbing his neck in his hands the way he did when he was contemplating something difficult. He shook his head. "Shang Ik, we did send word to your *appa* today. It will be a while before we get a response. But I must tell you, child, that what you are asking may not be possible. It is very dangerous to cross the border between the North and the South right now. It's possible that you may not be able to leave."

Another aunt stood up quietly from the table. "Oh, Shang Ik, wouldn't you like to live with us here? You can still go to your school and have all your same friends. Your family is here, and when things settle down, your *appa* can come for you then."

The shaking of the boy's head and his resolute "No!" interrupted her.

He made his way toward the bedroom and then turned sharply in the doorway to address his relatives. "Thank you, but I only want to go with *Appa*. Please, *Jageun Appa*, tell him to send for me. I'm ready to go with him."

With that Shang Ik turned and entered his bedroom. Then he closed the door behind him. He climbed into the bed and pulled the sheet tightly over him as his family continued their discussion. He felt his body collapse from the exhaustion of this day. He had no idea how he would make it to the South. He did not know if his *appa* would come get him or if he would be sent on his own.

All he knew was that he would not be taking no for an answer, not from his uncles and aunts and not even from his own father. He had no more energy in his aching heart or tired mind for tears. He simply stared out the window of the small wooden room into the night sky until sleep mercifully overcame him.

Escape to Seoul

A pair of chocolate-colored eyes sprung open at the unmistakable crunch of rustling leaves and snapping twigs. Shang Ik stayed still until his eyes slowly grew accustomed to the dark around him. As they did, figures moving about in the shadows became clearer, and the rustling of hushed movements became more distinct.

In the dark, Shang Ik raised his head and sat up to his elbows, shaking his head as if trying to make sense of where he was. A gust of cold wind rushed over him, and the nip of the frost brought his memory back clear and sharp. Quickly he stood to his feet, quietly rolled up his mat, and secured it to his small pack. The other twenty or so people who had been asleep next to him were already packed up and gathering in a small huddle, ready to move at a moment's notice.

It had been several months since *Halmeoni*'s death. Against their better judgment, his relatives smuggled a message to his father in Seoul, detailing Shang Ik's request to be sent to live with him. The few days it took to await a response were the longest days in young Shang Ik's life.

The day the response finally did arrive brought with it another crushing reality for the boy. This would not be the exciting adventure he had been naïvely hoping for. Shang Ik's uncle sat him down at the table in their ancestral home one afternoon after Shang Ik came home from school and showed him the message that came from his father.

Brother,

I am saddened to hear of the passing of our mother. It was my desire to have been present at such a difficult time, but as you know that was not possible. Please give my condolences to our family and my warmest hug to my son. How I wish I could have been with him.

Although I have not wanted to embark on this risk in the past, I believe the time has come to resolve our unfortunate situation. Shang Ik and I have been separated for far too long.

I have made arraignments for a guide to smuggle Shang Ik across the 38th parallel. This man has done this before, and he already has a group of people prepared to leave. I will be waiting for Shang Ik once he reaches Seoul.

Please prepare him for this journey, as it will be more difficult than he anticipates. I will await your response.

Chun-Soo

Shang Ik beamed at the news. At first his heart sunk when he realized his father wouldn't come for him. But this seemed like the more exciting way to go. He was already mentally preparing a list of the exciting things he would share with his father about his journey. Eagerly he ran to his room, wanting to pack all his belongings that very moment, and quickly made quite a mess of his things trying to prepare himself.

His uncle followed him into his room and interrupted the boy in a pile of all his childish belongings.

"*Jageun Appa*, how will I carry all my things? Will we have a horse? Maybe I can hold some things in my hand while the horse carries the rest." Shang Ik looked around at his belongings and shook his head, brainstorming his trip.

His uncle took a wooden train out of his hands and sat the boy on his bed. At his uncle's words, Shang Ik's shoulders slumped, and his excitement began to leave him.

"This is a very dangerous journey, Shang Ik. You have to sneak into the South. That means no one must know you are coming. You have to quietly go by night, and you can't take things with you that will slow you down."

Shang Ik took in the room, staring at the eclectic collection of knickknacks he had accumulated in his ten years.

His uncle continued. "Once you get close to the border, there will be guards with guns. You'll have to sneak past them. They don't want people from the North just walking into the South and vice versa, especially these days. They will shoot anyone who attempts to make it across. If you see those guards, I want you to hide. Do you understand?"

Shang Ik's eyes widened at his uncle's solemn words. *Surely he didn't mean it would be that dangerous.*

His uncle got up from the bed and crouched before the boy, putting both his hands on his shoulders and speaking sternly. "I want you to always remember these words that I am telling you, Shang Ik. Keep them in your mind and repeat them to yourself every day. You do not let those guards see you under any circumstances. Is that clear? Whatever you do, you must never let them see you."

The boy nodded his head quickly, wanting to reassure his uncle that he understood his concerns. Inside he wasn't so sure. *I'm sure it won't be as bad as Jageun Appa thinks it will. He just doesn't realize how much I've grown. I'm not a little boy anymore. I'll show him.*

Shang Ik continued to anticipate this surreptitious trip with childish naïveté, whereas his uncle spent the better part of the next few months lecturing the boy about precautions he should take during the journey. When he wasn't reminding him about guards and light towers, he was taking him out into the woods to teach him some basic survival skills.

"Remember, in case you get lost or lose your group, Shang Ik, and you want to know which way is south, in the morning when you wake up, where the sun is, that's east. If you stretch your two hands out, whichever way your right hand points is south. Now stretch out your hands."

Shang Ik obediently stretched out his hands in the morning sun, feeling silly as his uncle nodded with satisfaction.

Weeks later Shang Ik was grateful for those lessons as he stood in the center of a huddle of strangers in the middle of the night in the deep wilderness. As the guide who was in command gave instructions in a loud whisper, the boy's face reddened under the shifty glances of the many weary sojourners who made up this group. Their faces were young and old, some wrinkled and others haggard and scruffy. But they shared a similar glint of fear in their eyes, similar expressions of mistrust and anxious tension as they trusted their lives to a stranger, not knowing if they would survive the harrowing journey they were on together.

Shang Ik had already been caught lagging behind, and several times the large group of people had to slow down their pace and wait for the boy to catch up to them. Although his father paid the man a substantial amount to convey his son across the border, the guide was quickly losing his patience with the boy.

Several times Shang Ik had been so exhausted that he had fallen asleep while still walking. He could have fallen and broken a bone or cried out and alerted a sentry. The guide had to nudge the boy with his elbow to wake him up. They simply didn't have the luxury to stop or slow down because the boy couldn't keep up the pace.

Shang Ik was too anxious to be fully embarrassed by the negative attention he was attracting from the others in the group. When he wasn't forcing himself to stay awake and attentive, he was busy scouring the horizon for the guarded light towers his uncle warned him about.

He was so tense that he couldn't sleep during their designated rest times, which meant he couldn't keep his eyes open when it was time for the group to move on. Even now, while the guide whispered his intense warnings, the boy's eyelids were heavy with sleep as he struggled to stay awake.

"Remember, we are almost near the border. That means there are guarded light towers at checkpoints all along this path. We need to stay together, keep quiet, and keep up the pace. No more lagging behind. We won't be stopping for anymore stragglers." With those words, the stern man's eyes fell on Shang Ik.

The boy's face turned a bright crimson as he tightened his grip on his pack and ignored their stares.

The man nodded his head and addressed the entire group one final time. "We are almost there, so keep a steady, quick pace. Ready? Let's go."

The large huddle moved forward slowly, sneaking quietly, staying low, and going from tree to tree and bush to bush. Everyone was marching with a mixture of fear and heightened adrenaline. The hours passed, but the tension never subsided. They passed one guarded light tower about an hour into their march.

The guide let out his signal, an owl's hoot, and the entire group dropped onto the icy ground. As they did, a large beam of light traveled slowly above their heads. Shang Ik closed his eyes, wanting to sink into the earth beneath him. The cold seeped through his clothing, making it impossible to slow his heartbeat. A few minutes later, another owl hoot told the group it was safe to stand up and resume the harrowing march.

With each passing hour, Shang Ik struggled to stay awake. Several times his eyes closed, and he slipped into a light sleep while his legs kept moving forward. He would realize he was asleep only when he tripped over his own feet or ran into the back of a small woman or older man who would give him an angry shove to wake him up.

Several times that night, Shang Ik would open his eyes to find that the group was already several paces in front of him. Terrified, he would pump his arms and legs to catch up, his breath coming out in halting puffs into the cold night air.

All night the group traveled until they were near the border. They took a ten-minute rest, and the guide informed them that they would cross the border by the middle of the night and be at Seoul by early morning. This ten-minute rest was meant to invigorate them, but Shang Ik could not overcome his exhaustion.

Every time he had to continue marching after those rests was torturous for the boy. There were no other children in the group, and no one seemed concerned that he might need to travel at a different speed than the adults with him. In times of danger, patience and wisdom go out the window. There was only the moment and their shared need to survive this journey, no matter the cost.

As they neared the border, Shang Ik felt himself slipping again into unconsciousness. Despite the cold, his eyes crossed as his eyelids became heavy. He shook his head, trying to stay awake, until his vision turned to flying birds and soaring mountain ranges. He pictured himself flying over the top of the group, above the light towers, and into his father's waiting arms.

Just as he was beginning his descent into a bustling colorful city, a sharp sound cracked like a whip, and his eyes sprung open. Shang Ik froze where he stood and slowly lowered his eyes toward his feet, his heart sinking into his stomach.

Beneath him was a frozen river, glistening and perfect, except for the giant crack in the ice just beneath his right foot. The boy's breath became shallow as he slowly glanced up, hoping that someone—anyone—had heard the sound of the ice cracking and would be coming to help him. His heart raced uncontrollably at the realization that the group had moved far ahead of him after he had fallen asleep on his feet. A shift in the ice beneath him caused him to open his mouth in a scream, but no sound came out.

A rush of frigid water swallowed his scream, as his head submerged hopelessly into the icy depths. The frozen water assaulted his skin like thousands of pinpricks while his arms and legs flailed in four different directions. No amount of training could have prepared Shang Ik for the terror that consumed his mind as he helplessly struggled under the dark water. Every organ in his body rebelled against the cold. He couldn't swim.

Shang Ik's panic gave way to sudden relief when his foot touched something solid. Through the panic, he realized he could reach the bottom of the river. He planted both feet and propelled himself to the surface, taking a deep breath that stabbed his lungs with freezing cold air. Still the water came to his chin. He took a few more deep breaths as tears froze on his cheeks.

He stopped flailing his arms to cease the mini waves he was sending toward his face. Trembling and mostly submerged in the freezing water, he looked around, his teeth chattering behind blue lips. He slowly began to move forward toward the riverbank.

Inch by inch he crept, measuring each step tentatively with his toe before he moved forward. Terrified that the bottom would drop off and he would sink to his death, he moved only a centimeter at a time, each step shrouded with dread. Through the thin light of a clouded moon, Shang Ik could make out the edge of the river. With his last step, his outstretched arm grasped a rock on the bank.

A light layer of frost glistened on the river's edge as his arm plopped onto the bank. He pulled himself out of the water, clawing up the riverbank on his elbows and knees. Once out of the water, his clothes immediately became like a sheet of ice. His breath was halting as tears flowed freely, stinging his eyes and freezing onto his lashes.

He sat there for only a moment, his entire body trembling. Slowly he raised his head, and through the tears, he could make out the outline of the group of people walking far ahead of him. *I...I have to keep moving. I have to get up.*

His childish desire to wait for someone to come for him was quietly snatched away by the reality that the group was getting farther and farther away. He stared desperately into the night, wondering if there were any chance they would notice he was missing. He shook his head desperately, realizing he could not wait for someone to come for him.

Shang Ik stood on shaking legs and trembling knees and began to slowly jog toward the shadows he could make out only by a glint of moonlight. He picked up the pace, generating enough heat to melt the ice off his clothing.

A minute or two of light jogging caught him up with the rest of the group. As he neared the huddle, he made his way toward the guide, unsure of how to tell him what had happened.

"Sir...excccuse me. I fffell into the..."

"Shhhh!" The guide shushed the soaking-wet boy and motioned for the entire group to crouch down into the dirt.

Shang Ik stood in the center of the huddle of bone-weary travelers, his hair and clothes still dripping wet. No one in the group seemed to notice as they all stared attentively at the guide. Shang Ik slowly lowered himself to the ground, but his heart would not slow its beating.

The guide spoke in a loud whisper. "All right, everyone. This is it. The light towers are all along this ridge here, and they have a wide girth. Let's pass through five at a time. Remember to be as silent and stealthy as you can. There are men with guns in all those towers. You make noise at your own risk."

There was a general murmur as the people in the group gathered themselves and prepared to cross. Shang Ik kept his hand over his chest, trying to steady his breathing. He had nothing to gather. What little belongings he brought with him were at the bottom of a frozen river. The guide grabbed the boy's hand away from his chest and pulled him to his side. He silently motioned with his hand for three more to follow him and the rest to wait until they passed.

After the first rotation of the searchlight from a nearby tower passed them, their group moved quietly. The guide dragged Shang Ik by the arm with little regard to the discrepancy in their sizes. They passed the guarded towers undetected and then waited for the entire group to catch up with them.

They continued traveling as a frozen sun rose in the sky, relieved they no longer had to hide under cover of nightfall. They had passed the last border tower and were now safely in the territory of South Korea. Little by little, members of the group drifted off to stay in one town or another. Shang Ik and the guide pressed forward until they reached the city of Seoul Eui-Jung-Boo, where a prearranged truck was waiting for the rest of the group to be transported to Seoul.

Shang Ik's father had sent word that he would be waiting for him at the entrance of a designated location in the city. Shang Ik had imagined that meeting with great anticipation, but now with the memory of his own near drowning still fresh and the experience of having taken such a perilous and tense journey, Shang Ik did not know how to feel. He was emotionally drained.

He allowed himself to be blindly led, sometimes dragged, by this callous guide, and as they entered the bustling city of Seoul, his breathing again became halting. But he had made it. As he entered Seoul, worse for wear but alive, he was struck by how strange he felt. He knew now why his uncle had warned him so sternly of this journey. Surely many others had not made it through alive.

It felt strange to him suddenly to be walking freely in South Korea after traveling a path that had taken so many other lives. Shang Ik was overwhelmed with a heavy mixture of gratitude, guilt, and relief. Considering he was also utterly exhausted, he wasn't capable of processing any of those emotions.

The people, trolleys, businesses, bicycles, and several different vehicles were more than the boy had anticipated. The guide dragged him through the streets as the boy struggled to keep up the pace. Merchants shouted, children ran energetically through busy roads, policemen directed traffic, and cars, bicycles, and trolleys fought for territory on the large streets. Shang Ik was forcibly maneuvered through busy traffic and an overwhelming symphony of sights, sounds, and smells. The guide deposited him onto a street corner and told the boy to wait there while he searched for his father.

Alone on the street corner, Shang Ik felt even more perplexed. *What will my life be like here? What will my future be in a place like this?* People bustled about him continuously, hustling through their busy day. He tried to remain calm but could not stop himself from jumping at every loud sound or from darting his eyes back and forth at all the movement. This was not his *halmeoni*'s sleepy little village.

The minutes crawled by slowly as the boy waited for his father. With each passing moment, he wondered if he had been abandoned to the streets and would have to find his own way to his *appa*. *How will Appa find me in all this? Should I look for him? No, he told me to wait here. I'll wait a few minutes longer. But what if he doesn't know where to come find me? Maybe if I just...*

"Shang Ik?" His father's voice cracked like a whip through the noises of the crowd, silencing the questions in Shang Ik's mind and the fear in his heart.

The bustle of the crowded city became like white noise as the boy slowly turned toward the sound of his father's voice calling his name. One look told Shang Ik everything he needed to know about his father's desire and intentions for him.

Chun-Soo stood there in the midst of crowds of people teeming about him to and fro. Tears flowed freely down his cheeks as he clutched at his heart with one hand. He took a few steps forward, using his other hand to push through the people.

Shang Ik felt like the tension he had been holding in his little body suddenly released, propelling him toward his father like the blast from a rocket ship. In a few short steps, father and son collided, the boy heaving as tears flowed uncontrollably and the father dropping to his knees with total abandon, rocking his son back and forth in his arms.

They stayed that way for a few minutes, quietly rocking in each other's arms until their tears subsided. Shang Ik's father gently pulled away and took a handkerchief out of his pocket to wipe his son's face and then his own. The little boy's breath came in halting movements as his father gently wiped his face. Both took deep breaths, and his father smiled.

"Come along, my son. Let's go home."

Chun-Soo stood to his feet, pulling his little boy up by his shoulders. Together they walked down the busy streets of Seoul, hand in hand, this time neither of them caring if the whole world saw them cry.

Seoul-ful

Twelve-year-old Shang Ik awoke in the middle of the night with a shout, his pillow moist with sweat, his heart beating thunderously in his chest. Panting, he looked around him. His vision shifted between snowy riverbanks and bedroom furniture. Eventually the snowy bank retreated to his subconscious, and he became fully awake, realizing he was in his bedroom in Seoul.

He slowly inhaled, trying to shake the images of murky freezing water and the feeling of tightness in his chest. A light just outside his door told him he had woken his *appa* and *uibus-eomi*. He tried quickly to wipe the sweat off his face with the sleeve of his pajama as his *uibus-eomi* entered the room, holding a glass of water.

"Shang Ik? Are you all right?" She came and sat on the edge of the bed, putting her hand on her stepson's chest.

Shang Ik nodded, but his stepmother's face showed she knew what had woken him up.

"Did you have another bad dream?"

Shang Ik nodded his head. His eyes shifted to his mattress.

"Was it the light towers or the river?" She handed him the glass.

He took a few large sips and waited until his breathing steadied before he answered. "The river. It's almost always the river."

Uibus-Eomi nodded. Concern filled her face. Shang Ik finished his water and set the glass on the night table. She put both hands on his face and smiled. "You haven't had these bad dreams for a long time. Not like when you first came home. Don't worry, my child. You are home. You are safe. Soon your mind will forget, and you won't have nightmares anymore."

Shang Ik nodded his head, shifting back under the covers. She seemed so convinced. He wasn't so sure.

His stepmother moved the hair out of his eyes and tightened the cover around him. "Goodnight, Shang Ik. Sleep well."

"Goodnight, *Uibus-Eomi.*"

She caressed his face lightly and then left the room. Alone in the dark again, Shang Ik could not fall asleep so easily.

It had been two years since he had arrived in Seoul to be with his father and stepmother. He quickly adjusted to life in a metropolitan urban environment and quite preferred it to the quiet village where he lived with

Halmeoni. He was able to catch up with his grade-school education at Duksoo Elementary School and was now enrolled in Whi-Moon High School, where he made many close friends in spite of his Northern dialect and customs.

When he first arrived to his *appa*'s new home, he was very anxious about how his new *uibus-eomi* would receive him. *Was she just pretending in all her letters? Would she be cold toward me? Was it safe to love her and care for her like Halmeoni had?*

His new *uibus-eomi* quickly put all his fears at ease. She loved her new son and treated him with warmth and kindness. She was tender and gentle and lavished him with love and support. They spent many hours together those first few months, just talking and getting to know each other. Shang Ik soon began to feel as if she had been his *uibus-eomi* all along, and it was Chun-Soo's favorite hobby to watch his new wife and his son together.

Shang Ik's older sister, Soon-Ja, lived not too far away with her husband, Jong-Pil Kim. Shang Ik hadn't known much about her except for her letters, but now that they were near each other, he spent a lot of time with his sister and new brother-in-law. Shang Ik had been worried that coming to Seoul would mean being away from the love of his family, but he had been willing to sacrifice that if it meant being with his father at last.

How he rejoiced when he realized he had been welcomed to Seoul by a family larger and more loving than he had ever expected, a family who had longed for him and wanted as desperately to have him with them as he had wanted to be with them.

Despite the welcome relief of adjusting easily to life in Seoul, psychological trauma still marred Shang Ik's time there. His first week he could not sleep unless his *appa* was in the room with him. Every time he closed his eyes, he heard gushing water and felt the cold on his skin. He simply could not forget his near-death experience, and he lost many nights of sleep avoiding the memories of that dreadful moment.

He dreamed every night of drowning in murky depths. Visions of his own frozen carcass haunted him day and night. The tension never left him. When he wasn't dreaming specifically about drowning, visions of light towers, guards with guns, and a general state of tension and harm tormented his sleep.

But as the first year passed, the dreams came more sparingly, and eventually Shang Ik was able to return to normalcy. He loved being with his parents, and he grew to enjoy the city of Seoul. There was always something to do, and he enjoyed the atmosphere of the big city. Life in his home and with his family and friends could not get any better. However, outside of the cocoon of family, a storm was brewing.

There were rumors that North Korea was preparing an invasion and had been since the end of the Second World War. Of course, Shang Ik's *appa* assured them they were just rumors and nothing substantial would happen without the South Korean government knowing about it. The Russian government had been collaborating with the communist-led North Korean People's Army, which was creating a lot of anxiety over the threat of war.

The democratic United States supported South Korea, and the clash between communism and democracy meant that the Korean people existed with an underbelly of tension. There was suspicion that many people who lived in South Korea were actually communist sympathizers. Because he worked for the government of South

Korea, Chun-Soo insisted that his family treat his work with total discretion. They did not discuss his government job with anyone outside of Shang Ik's *uibus-eomi*, Shang Ik, Soon-Ja, and Jong-Pil, a police section chief in Seoul.

The next morning Shang Ik rose from bed, feeling like he hadn't slept at all. After he dressed, he came into the kitchen area where his father sat, reading the morning paper. As his son trudged into the room, looking as haggard as a twelve-year-old can appear, Chun-Soo smiled sympathetically and set the paper down onto the table. Shang Ik rubbed the sleep out of his eyes and avoided his *appa*'s gaze. He always felt a little embarrassed when he woke up screaming or crying from a nightmare.

He shuffled away to the counter and mumbled a quick greeting. "Good morning, *Appa*." Shang Ik cut an apple and a slice of bread and sat at the table, silently picking at his breakfast.

Chun-Soo watched as his son kept his head down and his shoulders slumped. Quietly Chun-Soo pushed his chair back and walked over to the counter, whistling a simple melodic tune. With his hands in his pockets, he stood whistling, as if he took no notice of the sullen teenager at the table. Shang Ik, meanwhile, continued picking crumbs off his bread with his chin resting on his other hand.

After a few moments of whistling his tune, Chun-Soo slowly turned and moved nonchalantly behind his son's chair. Shang Ik raised his eyes from his pathetic breakfast and momentarily sat up. As he did, his father clapped him on the shoulders and began to shake him, just as he had when Shang Ik was a boy.

At first Shang Ik rolled his eyes and tried to pull away, groaning with annoyance. But he didn't try too hard, and his father kept shaking his shoulders, laughing as he did, until Shang Ik could not help but laugh at how silly he looked. His father continued shaking his shoulders for a few moments before wrapping his arms around him and hugging his boy, squeezing him tightly as he leaned over the back of his chair. Shang Ik smiled as he let his father hug him, this time not pulling away.

After that Shang Ik felt much better, and he and his father enjoyed a chat about Shang Ik's sports team and an upcoming test in school as they finished breakfast. They began every morning this way, chatting over breakfast and then walking together toward Shang Ik's school. They separated on the road that led to the Capitol Building where Chun-Soo worked.

As time had passed, the government of South Korea had accepted Shang Ik's father as a valued part of the development of the new country. He had an important role to play, and he took it very seriously.

As they neared the point in the road where they parted ways, father and son walked together for a few minutes in silence. They also slowed their pace, as they always did before they reached that point, as if prolonging the moment when they would have to separate, even if only by a few minutes.

"Shang Ik, don't forget to stop by your *azumma*'s tailor shop today after school. She wants you to pick up your high school uniform that she tailor-made for you. Be sure to thank her."

Shang Ik nodded, glad for the reminder. *Azumma* was a tailor whom his father had introduced him to a few months earlier. She and his father seemed to be old friends, and his father made their introduction a very important event.

At first Shang Ik wasn't sure why it mattered that he get to know this woman who was a tailor and made clothes, but he was glad now that he had met her. She was always eager to see him. She always laid out treats and snacks for him after school.

When he went to see her to get his first suit, they ended up chatting for hours, and before long it was like they were old friends. She always asked Shang Ik to visit her when he got out of school, and he usually spent an hour or so with her before he went home for the evening. She had become like a second mother to him, and Shang Ik was not one to dismiss any extra motherly affection. He had even taken to calling her *eomma-azumma*, as a gesture of affection for her motherly attention. She seemed to welcome the nickname.

"Don't stay too long at your *azumma*'s shop today, Shang Ik. I want you to come straight home once you pick up your uniform because I have an important meeting after work and I won't be home until late. I want you to be home right away to help your *uibus-eomi* until I get there."

"Are you meeting today in the Secret Garden, *Appa*?" Shang Ik asked with eager curiosity.

"Hush!" His father quickly looked around, but no one was within earshot. He pulled his son close to him. "I've told you repeatedly. You must make sure no one can hear you when we speak of my work or anything to do with the government. We don't know who can be trusted these days."

Shang Ik nodded and darted his eyes around. Then he lowered his voice to a whisper. "But will you be discussing the war?"

Chun-Soo looked around and then shook his head. "Shang Ik, there is no war. Not yet. And all this worry and fuss everyone is making over it isn't helping any. We should just stay calm and focus on being good citizens. That's all anyone can do right now."

They stopped as they approached the point where Shang Ik turned toward his school.

"*Appa*?"

"Yes, Shang Ik."

"But do you think there is going to be a war?"

His father's eyes remained fixed on the ground for a long pause before he raised his head and sighed deeply. "Let's hope it doesn't come to that, my boy. There would be nothing worse."

He departed from his son with a sad smile and a pat on the shoulder. Shang Ik watched his father's dark figure as it faded into the shadow of government buildings. Then he turned and went down the road that led to his school.

Late that afternoon Shang Ik raced from school down the street that led to his *azumma*'s house. He rushed past the shouts from local merchants selling their goods and sped by the police officer directing traffic, ignoring the shrill whistle warning him to stay off the main road. *Eomma-Azumma probably has the dumplings all ready by now.*

Lately his father had been asking Shang Ik to stop by *Eomma-Azumma*'s home for various errands...more than usual. However, Shang Ik didn't mind. In fact he enjoyed going there after school because she always prepared delicious snacks for him. Besides, *Eomma-Azumma* seemed to enjoy these visits more than Shang Ik did. She would always stop what she was doing to soak in all the boy's chitchat, quizzing him about his daily life.

Like any normal preadolescent, movement and food were his primary concerns. He bounded up the steps to his *eomma-azumma*'s home, making record time. He entered the house red-faced just as his *eomma-azumma* was placing steaming hot dumplings into a basket.

"Oh, Shang Ik, there you are! I was wondering what took you so long."

She teased him gently, knowing by his red face that he had run straight from school. As he stood there panting, she shook her hands at him. "Wash that face and those hands right now before you sweat all over my food!"

Shang Ik laughed as he caught the towel she tossed his way. He ran to the outside courtyard to wash his face in the water pump.

"Did you not walk home with your father today?" *Eomma-Azumma* asked when he ran inside, his face barely dry.

Shang Ik plucked two dumplings off the basket and was ready to snatch a third when she slapped his hand. She then turned toward the stew that was simmering on the stove.

Turning her head to see what the boy was up to, she chided him. "Shang Ik! That is no way to eat dinner. Sit down! You should wait for your father to come by."

Shang Ik swallowed quickly. "*Appa* won't be home until late today. He has another meeting." He lowered his voice and whispered conspiratorially, "In the Secret Garden."

Eomma-Azumma quickly nodded and changed the subject, as she often did when they were discussing his father's government job. "Tell me, Shang Ik. What did you learn in school today?"

"Well, they had a man come in to talk to us about our futures, about what we want to be when we grow up. We all had to stand up in front of the class and give our answers."

She nodded as she continued preparing her meal. "And what did you say you wanted to be?"

"I want to be an atomic scientist!"

Eomma-Azumma quickly turned toward him, her hands still deftly stirring her stew. "What? What made you want to be such a thing?"

"Well, everyone remembers the atomic bomb the Americans dropped at Hiroshima. It was a massive explosion! It would be such fun to build one someday. I would like to make something that powerful."

She silently stirred the stew as she listened to Shang Ik discuss weapons of mass destruction with cavalier amusement. She too remembered the carnage at Hiroshima. "Shang Ik, atomic bombs destroy things. They hurt people. Wouldn't you like to be something that helps people? Like a doctor! Doctors save lives and help people who are sick."

She turned just in time to catch him making faces at her suggestion.

She chuckled. "Or how about a lawyer? Your father always says you can argue your way out of almost every predicament. I'm sure he wants you to be a lawyer someday like him. Wouldn't you like that?"

Shang Ik's face contorted even further. Then his eyebrows shot up as he excitedly sat up in his seat. "*Eomma-Azumma*, I almost forgot to tell you all about my dream!"

She pulled the wooden spoon to her mouth to taste her stew. With a satisfied nod, she removed the kettle from the flame and then came to the table to sit down. "Now what was this dream, Shang Ik?"

"The other night I dreamed that you were actually my mother! As we walked with my hand in yours, you dropped my hand, speeding away into a distant horizon while I was yelling out, *Eomma! Eomma!* Then you disappeared like a dot into the far horizon. I stood there alone, crying and crying, but no one would hear me. That woke me up." Shang Ik shrugged his shoulders as if there were nothing else to say. Then he swiftly popped another dumpling into his mouth.

As he enjoyed the dumpling, closing his eyes and reveling in the flavor, *Eomma-Azumma* turned and lowered her head, blinking her eyes to stop her tears from falling. She stood quickly and turned again toward her stew, using the dishtowel to wipe her eyes. "Finish those dumplings, Shang Ik. I'll go get your uniform so you can go home to your *appa* and *uibis-eomma*."

Appa

Sunday mornings were Shang Ik's favorite day of the week. There was no school, and most of his household chores had been done the day before. *Appa* wouldn't work most Sundays, and it would just be Shang Ik and his *appa* and *uibis-eomi*. They would often take Sunday morning strolls or go to the market. Many Sunday evenings they spent at his sister Soon-Ja's house with her husband and little children. But his favorite Sunday pastime was a family outing to Chang-Kyung-Won, his favorite park in Seoul.

"What are we going to do today, *Appa*?" Shang Ik yelled from inside his room as he ripped off his pajamas and put on play clothes.

His father appeared in the doorway, and Shang Ik stopped dressing when he noticed his father was dressed for work.

Shang Ik's shoulders slumped, and he let out an exasperated grunt. "Not again! Besides this is Sunday!"

Chun-Soo smiled sympathetically and came into the room. "I'm sorry, Shang Ik. I have another meeting today at the Secret Garden."

"But I thought we could go to the park together." Shang Ik grit his teeth, clearly gearing up for a whine.

But Chun-Soo's jovial smile and the sense that he too seemed disappointed quickly disarmed Shang Ik. *I'm getting too old to whine anyway. I should act mature, like Appa is.*

"Well, we'll be up for it another time, hmm?" Chun-Soo said, gently touching his son's hair. "Make sure you finish all your homework and be good for your *uibis-eomi*."

"I always am," Shang Ik said with slight indignation and a puff of his twelve-year-old shoulders.

Chun-Soo chuckled at that as he left the room. "We'll see about that when I get home later today."

Shang Ik followed his father out the front door and leaned against it as his father walked toward the path that led to his job. Chun-Soo walked a few paces down the road. Then he turned and wiggled his shoulders at Shang Ik and laughed.

Shang Ik laughed too, erupting into a spastic wiggle of his own as he waved his father off. "See you later, *Appa!*"

Shang Ik spent the rest of the morning lounging about in his room until early afternoon when *Uibis-Eomi* called him in for lunch. The growing boy scarfed down his meal with the vigor of someone who had just put in twelve hours of hard labor, as opposed to a boy who had spent the better part of the last few hours contemplating whether he would grow quicker if he did stretching exercises before bed.

Uibis-Eomi smiled at Shang Ik as she set another plate before him. Swinging his feet underneath the table, he chewed his food with gusto as he convinced himself that he was only an inch or two away from touching the bottom. *Maybe Appa will get out of his meeting early enough that we'll still have time to go to the park before dark.*

Three curt taps on the door snapped him out of his reverie. Shang Ik and his *uibus-eomi* paused for a moment, both staring at the door. *Uibis-Eomi* stood quickly, wiping her hands on her dishtowel.

She approached the door and opened it a crack. "Yes?"

A police officer stood in the doorway, holding his hat in his hands. Shang Ik stood from the table, trying to peer past *Uibus-Eomi* to see clearly.

The officer spoke curtly. "Are you Myung-Ja, wife of Chun-Soo Moon?"

At the mention of his father's name, Shang Ik rushed to stand next to *Uibis-Eomi* in the doorway.

She quickly answered, "Yes, I am Myung-Ja, and Chun-Soo is my husband."

The police officer lowered his voice to a more respectful low tone. "I am so sorry to inform you that your husband was taken to the hospital today. He suffered a stroke while at a meeting. Those at the meeting rushed him to the hospital, but it was too late. He has passed away."

The officer kept mumbling information to the woman about times, conditions, and names of those who had been present in case they wanted to contact someone. At that point, however, none of his words was making any sense. They landed on the ground like feathers or dust, airy and ethereal. *What was he saying? Something about a morgue?*

The little boy backed away from his *uibuseomi* at the door—back, back, back until he hit a wall and could retreat no further. He placed his palms on the wall behind him to steady himself and keep off the crushing weight of fear.

Meanwhile *Uibis-Eomi* had forced herself to nod when the police officer asked if she understood, shaking her head bravely when he asked if she needed anything further from him. He bowed his head and placed his officer's cap back on, signifying he was satisfied that his work here was done.

Uibis-Eomi watched as the officer walked away, as if she were holding off on closing the door. She waited still longer after he had gone, staying there in the doorway. The evening sky began to cast its shadows on the houses and rooftops. Suddenly, as if she just remembered, she turned to look for Shang Ik.

There he was, still and small against the back wall. He had been growing tall, and just this morning, she remarked to her husband how tall he was becoming. But in that moment, with his back pressed against the wall, his face white, his eyes wide, and his chest heaving up and down quickly, he looked tiny.

She closed the door slowly and then walked toward Shang Ik. His chest was heaving more and more, and his stomach was now moving with the motion of the intense breaths he was taking. She knelt before the boy, this little boy whom she considered her child, and lightly placed her hand on his chest. She looked down, trying to compose herself. Then she looked up at him. Their eyes met, and she could not hold back her tears.

"Shang Ik, my son," she began.

Then the words were cut off. Her eyes lowered, and her head and shoulders stooped. She kept one hand on Shang Ik's chest, another balled up in a fist near her stomach. She shook her head, unable to find the words out of her own broken heart to comfort Chun-Soo's child.

Tears flowed freely now as she struggled to compose herself. She broke, setting the hand at her stomach down onto the floor to steady herself. Her mind kept telling her to stay calm, to gather and compose herself for Shang Ik's sake, but her tears spilled out onto their kitchen floor like monsoon rains.

She felt a small hand touch her head. Slowly Shang Ik began to caress her hair, just like his father had done so many times. With her head still lowered to the floor, she reached both arms out and gathered Shang Ik into herself. The boy who had been so tall that morning and too old for nightmares last night folded into his *uibus-eomi*'s lap like a toddler and lay weeping with his head on her chest.

Appa. Appa. Appa. Shang Ik tried earnestly to grab onto a thought that made sense, one reflection that steadied him. *A stroke? What did that mean?* He knew it had something to do with the heart. *Or was it the brain? Did Appa suffer? Was he in pain? What will I do without him? Where will I go? Who will take care of them? Who will protect them? How will Appa stop the war now?*

Shang Ik's breathing turned shallow as his head began to hurt with the pressure of his own thoughts. *Had he said goodbye to Appa? Had they hugged?* The other day *Appa* hugged him in front of his school friends, and Shang Ik had pushed him away. *Did he know I was just kidding? He had to have known that I didn't really care. I'll tell him. I'll tell him tomorrow that I didn't care and that he can hug me whenever he wants. I'll tell him. I'll...*

The thoughts ceased as a wave of fresh realization washed over him. There would be no telling *Appa*. There would be no making it right. His sobs caught in his chest as he opened his mouth, but no sound came out. Gripping tightly onto *Uibus-Eomi*'s shirt, he squeezed, trying hard to fight against the current that was threatening to wash him away into despair, like the icy river of his nightmares.

Stepmother and stepson stayed on the kitchen floor for many hours, until the evening sun began to set. Eventually, his *uibus-eomi* raised herself and then helped Shang Ik off the floor.

She walked him toward the bedroom. "It is late. We will lay down and try to sleep."

Shang Ik climbed into his parents' bed on his father's side, while *Uibus-Eomi* lay down next to him. Tears continuously flowed, sometimes giving way to soft sobs. Eventually their bodies could no longer carry the weight of their grief, and the two exhausted souls drifted off to sleep.

An Unfortunate Arrangement

The next morning, Shang Ik's older sister, Soon-Ja, and her husband, Jong-Pil Kim, came to the house. Soon-Ja helped her *uibus-eomi* make arrangements for the funeral and tried to keep her little brother's spirits lifted even through her own tears. Shang Ik appreciated his sibling's efforts, but no amount of caring or distraction would lift the burden off his heart.

His brother-in-law, a section police chief in Seoul, would come to Shang Ik and invite him on walks around the city or offer to take him to the local market for a sweet treat, but Shang Ik always declined. The boy spent most days in his room, only venturing out for the funeral.

Korean funerals traditionally last for three days, culminating with the burial on the third day. It is also tradition that the eldest surviving male relative greets guests and symbolically acts as host of the event. It fell to Shang Ik to stand stoically in the doorway as people trickled in and out of the home, paying their respects. The women shed tears and outwardly expressed mourning, while the men stood calm and reserved, as was the custom.

Shang Ik learned to detach from his feelings as he stood in the doorway greeting guests. He plastered a neutral look on his face, not too weary, not too emotional. The guests entered into the home, buzzing around him in a haze of dark colors and whispered tones.

As he stood in the doorway with a blank expression, a small woman came into the home, carrying a single white orchid. Shang Ik's heart warmed as he immediately recognized his *eomma-azumma*.

She came to the boy and unashamedly pulled him into her arms for a hug. Shang Ik sank into her warm embrace even as her tears stained the new suit she had made for him. After a few moments, she pulled herself away and handed him the orchid.

"I won't stay, Shang Ik. This is a time for your family, and I won't intrude. But just know that you must continue coming to see me when you are ready. Come see me and we will talk like old times. Is that all right?"

Shang Ik nodded, still not trusting himself to speak. She peered at him intently through watery and bloodshot eyes, touching his cheek with her hand softly. Then she turned and walked away.

The rest of the ceremonial traditions seemed to go by quickly, but Shang Ik could not retain many of the moments that seemed so significant to people who were there. He was just counting down the time until he could once again be alone with his thoughts about his *appa*. There was nothing else he wanted to do.

After three days of burial traditions, Shang Ik and his *uibis-eomi* were finally allowed to process their grief in private. The boy and his *uibis-eomi* took turns comforting each other, each coming to the other's side when grief overwhelmed them. Shang Ik would often come into her room in the middle of the night, led there by her uncontrollable sobbing. Many nights he would wake to find her sitting next to his bed, holding his hand or rubbing his back, his wet pillow revealing that he had been crying in his sleep.

For several months Soon-Ja and Jong-Pil were frequent visitors in the home. The three adults spent many hours in whispered conversations while Shang Ik spent his time in his room. He did not venture out, and he took his time returning to school. The thought of that daily walk without *Appa* was enough to make him want to drop out of school altogether.

One evening when Shang Ik came out of his room and into the kitchen for something to eat, he saw Soon-Ja and Jong-Pil at the table, whispering with his *uibus-eomi*. The whispering ceased immediately when they saw the boy. Soon-Ja and Jong-Pil looked red-faced and uncomfortable. *Uibus-Eomi* had her hands folded in front of her on the table with her eyes closed.

"*Uibus-Eomi*?" Shang Ik came to his stepmother, putting his hand on her shoulder.

Her eyes opened, and she took Shang Ik by the hand. "Shang Ik, there is something I want to talk to you about."

Shang Ik sat in the empty seat at the table and looked at his sister. Soon-Ja smiled at him reassuringly.

Uibus-Eomi took a deep breath and turned to the boy. "Shang Ik, now that your father is gone, there are some matters that need to be taken care of."

Shang Ik shifted in his seat nervously.

Uibus-Eomi continued. "You see, Shang Ik, I can't care for you by myself anymore. I can't work and care for you here at home."

Shang Ik sat up straight as an arrow in the seat. "*Uibus-Eomi*, I can find a job. I can take care of us."

Uibus-Eomi shook her head vigorously. "No, my son, you must stay in school. You are just a child. You have to stay in school and study so that someday you can be a doctor, a lawyer, or even a nuclear scientist. That is why I want you to go live with your sister and her family."

Shang Ik sank into the chair, stunned. He slowly turned to look at his sister and her police officer husband.

Jong-Pil tried to smile and reassure the boy. He put his hand playfully on the boy's shoulder. "Come, Shang Ik. It will be all right. You'll come home with your sister and me, and we'll have fun, huh?"

His sister leaned forward and took her brother's other hand. "Shang Ik, we can come visit with *Uibis-Eomi* sometimes if you like. And she can come visit with us. This is not forever. This is only until you're a little older and can better care for yourself."

He wiped a hand across his eyes and put his head down. Two tears left wet tracks on his cheeks as they dropped onto his shirtfront. He started to open his mouth, but the words stuck behind his lips.

Silently Soon-Ja and Jong-Pil stood up from the table and went outside. His *uibus-eomi* said nothing for a few moments. She let her own tears fall. Then she scooted her chair closer to her distraught son and set her hand on his chest.

"Shang Ik, you know that I would keep you with me forever if I could, don't you? Your father did not make much money, but he supported us, and he took care of us. But now we have had no income for some time while our debts are piling up."

Shang Ik lifted his head slowly. His eyes were swimming with tears, which he manfully tried to hold back.

"But *Uibis-Eomi*, I can work. I don't have to go to school. I don't have to be a lawyer, a doctor, or anything. I can work for now and help you take care of us."

Uibus-Eomi managed a brief smile. Then she turned away toward the window. "Shang Ik, I think your father was wrong. I think a war is coming and soon. I don't know when or how, but I think something terrible is about to happen here in Seoul. And if it does, you may not have another opportunity to go to school. No chance to be a little boy. You may have to grow up very fast."

Shang Ik wiped his eyes with the back of his hand. He didn't understand what his *uibus-eomi* was saying. *But what does war have to do with me growing up? I won't be involved in any war.*

"I know this may seem strange to you. And I know you have had a difficult time understanding everything that has happened. But for now, I need you to trust your *uibus-eomi.* I need you to trust that I know best and I will do whatever it takes for you to be safe. Will you trust me? Will you go live with your sister for now until we can be together again?"

Shang Ik choked back his tears and swallowed the lump in his throat. "I will until I can help you find work, *Uibis-Eomi*. And I can work with you after school, and we can live together again soon."

She paused and lowered her head, as if what she was about to say caused her much pain. Shang Ik simply stared at her, placing his hand over the hand on his chest.

Uibis-Eomi looked up quickly and said through her tears, "Shang Ik, there is a man who offered to pay for all our debts and who wants to marry me. But he just wants it to be him and I. No…no children." With that, her voice choked, and she buried her head in her arms, sobbing.

Shang Ik pulled his hand away from hers and sat quietly as she sobbed. The realization of what was happening settled over him like a heavy curtain. *I'll be on the streets if I stay here. If she's willing to marry this man, it must be rough for her. I understand now why she wants me to leave. I do wish she had just chosen me, though. Why doesn't anyone ever just choose me?*

Her sobs began to subside as she wiped her eyes. Despair and guilt were etched onto her pretty face. Shang Ik sighed deeply. *I know she loved me, even if it was just for Appa's sake. And she didn't have to. So I should just let her go be happy. What else is there to do?*

He reached over and touched her hand. "Don't worry, *Uibus-Eomi.* I'll go live with my sister. I'll go to Soon-Ja, and I will come visit you. Maybe you can come visit me. Don't cry. Everything will work out fine. I'm going to go to my room now."

With that he pushed away from the table and walked into his room while his *uibus-eomi* sat at the kitchen table and wept.

North Korean People's Army

Shang Ik moved in with his sister and her family a few days after that. When he entered his sister's home that first day, he was struck by the variety of tiny statues strategically situated around the home. There were male, female, and all forms of animal deities. Some were large; others were medium sized. Many were small enough to set on a window ledge.

"Don't you dare lay a finger on any of those statues, dirty boy!"

A shrill voice startled Shang Ik. He stepped away from a small elflike figure he had been admiring by the doorway. Just then his sister walked into the room and stood beside the elderly woman who had issued the command.

"Shang Ik, you remember my mother-in-law, my husband's mother? *Eomeonim*, you remember my brother, Shang Ik."

The old woman sniffed at the boy and shuffled off into the other room.

Soon-Ja shrugged and smiled at her brother. "Never mind her, Shang Ik. Come. Let's unpack your things."

That evening Shang Ik lay in bed, thinking about Soon-Ja and Jong-Pil Kim's mother, how mean the old woman had been to him and how they had said evening prayers to several of their idols. *Why did they do that? What were they hoping to get from those stone beings? And why did Soon-Ja's mother-in-law so dislike me?* Every day he spent at his sister's house, he pondered the same questions.

In the morning, he would help his sister with her chores before he went to school, and in the afternoon he would keep his young nephew, Duk-Soo, entertained or help care for his baby niece. Most importantly he would try to stay out of the old woman's way. She was cranky, bitter, and spiteful. She resented Shang Ik's presence in their already crowded living space and made sure the boy knew it every chance she had.

The threat of war with the North was becoming more and more imminent, as evidenced by the changing atmosphere in the city of Seoul. Because of his father's position in the government, Shang Ik and his family had always taken precautions when it came to how they communicated with and related to their neighbors.

Knowing there was a possibility of invasion and occupation by North Korea, they also knew their family would be targeted if war ever did become a reality. Shang Ik's father told his family that the word from the capitol was that there was no expectation of war.

And if there were a war, the South Korean military leaders were confident that any invasion would be met with swift retaliation. They were confident in the size and scope of their forces.

Several months passed with the new family arrangement, with Shang Ik trying his best to spend as much time as possible away from his sister's house.

One day he and his friend, Seung-ik, were jogging near their school. They wandered slowly down the road, wasting time and talking about their day. As they dragged their feet to avoid their afternoon chores, they wandered down a narrow road lining a hillside, a favorite spot for young lovers to frequent. Something about the fields in the foreground and the quiet made it perfect for a secret rendezvous.

The boys trudged along in silence, Shang Ik especially dreading returning to his sister's and being confronted by her crotchety mother-in-law. In the distance, amid the chirping of the birds and the soft blowing of the summer wind, an intermittent popping sound could be heard. The noise was far off and sounded like someone dropping pebbles into a canyon in perfect rhythm.

"What is that sound?" Shang Ik wondered aloud.

Seung-ik shrugged his shoulders nonchalantly. "It's the wind."

Then as if to rebut his lazy conclusion, a resounding boom rattled the ground. It was a loud yet far-off boom, like an explosion or possibly a cannon.

"What was that?" Shang Ik exclaimed.

The boys ran up the nearest hill to get a better look at what was causing the noise. They reached the top and were immediately mesmerized at what they saw in the distance. Miles away, puffs of smoke could be seen accompanying each boom of the cannon fire.

The boys stood frozen at the sight of gunfire and explosions so close to them. Seung-ik shook his hands nervously. The hair on their arms stood straight up.

"They're close! They're so close!" Seung-ik's voice came out with a nervous squeak.

Shang Ik could only stare at the distant gunfire, rooted to the ground, unsure of what to do next. "They're still miles away. They won't reach us for another few days at least. Maybe they won't even come through here."

Seung-ik backed away from Shang Ik, stumbling down the hill as he called over his shoulder, "I've got to find my family, Shang Ik! Be careful! I'll see you later!"

Shang Ik stayed on that hilltop for a few more moments, mesmerized, trying to make out figures through the haze and distance. He turned slowly and began to jog down the hill and toward his sister's home as the cannon fire grew louder in the distance.

For two days, the noises of cannons in the distance resounded, but children were sent to school, and people went to work, waiting for a signal from the South Korean government about what they should be doing.

But unknown to the general population, the government had already evacuated many of its top people. Every important government official had secretly fled the city of Seoul, including their president, Syngman Rhee, leaving the rest of the population behind.

Once people got wind of that, many tried to escape Seoul across the Han River. Unknown to them, the South Korean officials had bombed the bridge that crossed the river to prevent the North Koreans from pursuing them further south. The attempt at military strategy proved fatal to many of their own citizens. Because they were not told that the bridge had been cut, many citizens perished as their vehicles plunged into the Han River as they tried to escape the city.

That night Shang Ik and Soon-Ja kept vigil at their house, waiting for Jong-Pil to come home. He never did. He had been absorbed by his policing duties south of the Han River and could not get word to his wife or mother. Soon-Ja was distraught over what had happened to her husband and could only hope that he was still alive.

Her mother-in-law used the occasion to pounce on Shang Ik with renewed fervor. "This little bad omen has come into our home to bring disaster. My son is missing because of him!"

Shang Ik looked to his sister to defend him, but she was staring out the window, her own eyes wide with concern.

As the North Koreans came closer, many of the communist sympathizers who had been in hiding in Seoul came out into the open. They had disguised themselves as friendly neighbors and businessmen, even teachers and policemen. But with the impending approach of the North Korean army and the fleeing of every South Korean government authority, these communist sympathizers began to openly harass their fellow citizens. They hounded those they felt would not cooperate with the communist way, threatening to turn them in to the North Korean soldiers once they had captured Seoul. In all the chaos that ensued during the three days it took for the North Koreans to invade Seoul, the children were summoned to return to school.

The communist army was already at the capital when Shang Ik and Seung-ik walked into their first class of the day. No teacher was present. Instead, in the front of the classroom stood several men in suits, demanding the children's attention. Shang Ik and his friend moved up close to hear the conversation.

"Come now, boys. We are looking for strong boys to join the Red Army! The Red Army will give you food and clothing and take good care of you. Everyone must join. You there! Sign here and join the Red Army."

One man grabbed the arm of a boy in the front row, encouraging him to sign his name to an agreement to join the army. Most of the boys stood frozen, unsure of how to respond. The men continued their pitch.

"The Red Army is the people's army! The Red Army is the power of the people.

Everyone must share the burden. Come join today!"

As the boys whispered and murmured among themselves, Seung-ik jabbed Shang Ik with his elbow and leaned over to whisper in his ear. "They're here recruiting for the Red Army! What should we do? What if they force us to join?"

Shang Ik shook his head and leaned over to his friend. "We can't agree to join their army. Their army is almost here. If we sign, there's no stopping them from taking us!"

The murmur in the room grew louder as the men in the front grew more aggressive.

"Boys! Communism is for the people! We will rule one day, and there will be only those who are with us and those who are against us. Join the Red Army! Now! Before it is too late."

Many of the boys began to sign a pledge to communism at the insistence of the men in the room.

Shang Ik shook his head and began to back away. He whispered to his friend, "Come on. Let's get out of here before he sees us. I'm not signing that pledge!"

Seung-ik nodded, and while the men in front were helping other boys sign their names to become soldiers, Seung-ik and Shang Ik crept out of the backdoor of the room. Once outside, they ran out of the courtyard, hopped over the fence, and did not stop until they reached their homes. Shang Ik ran straight, instinctively sprinting straight toward *Eomma-Azumma*'s home. He burst into the doorway, interrupting *Eomma-Azumma* as she made herself some tea.

"*Eomma-Azumma!*"

She jumped, and her teacup crashed onto the table. She stood quickly when she realized whom it was. "Shang Ik! What are you doing here? Why aren't you in school?" She tried quickly to gather the pieces of shattered teacup as she spoke.

Shang Ik hurried over to *Eomma-Azumma*, took the teacup shards out of her hand, and sat her down at the table. "*Eomma-Azumma*, some men were at the school today. They were telling all the boys to sign up to join the Red Army. They were telling us that communism is for the people and that if we are not with them, we are against them."

Eomma-Azumma slowly raised her hand to her mouth, and her face became pale.

Shang Ik continued. "Seung-ik and I managed to sneak out before anyone noticed, and we hopped over the fence and came straight home. What should I do? Can they force me to join the Red Army?"

Eomma-Azumma rose quickly from the table, her hand still covering her mouth. She paced around the kitchen while the boy watched her, waiting for guidance from her. After a few moments, their eyes met. Her hand slowly lowered from her mouth, and she came to sit down.

She took Shang Ik by the hand, staring into his face. Her eyes spilled over with sadness. "Shang Ik, I want you to run away."

Shang Ik pulled his hand away from hers. The blood drained from his face. "What! What do you mean run away?"

Eomma-Azumma continued, her voice insistent. "I want you to run away farther south. We've been wrong. Your father was wrong. He said the war wasn't coming, that the North would not invade. But they are already here. I went to the market today, and I kept hearing murmurs about people who will be turned in to the North Korean People's Army. Anyone who worked for the government is at risk. Because I knew your father, that includes me. I am already marked!"

Shang Ik shook his head in confusion. *How could this happen? Appa had been so certain.*

Eomma-Azumma picked up both his hands this time and held them tightly in hers. "Shang Ik, my boy, they may come for me. I know I'm in danger, but it's not too late for you. Just go south. Escape. Run away until you know for sure that you will be safe from danger."

"But *Eomma-Azumma...*" Shang Ik managed. "How can I go without you?"

She smiled a weak, sad grin. "You are a brave boy. You are growing into a strong young man. I have faith in you. I know you will manage. You must be strong now."

He looked down at the table, his eyes welling with tears at the thought of facing another journey alone. *How can I leave the only mother I have left? Uibus-Eomi* had given him up, and now he was being torn from his *eomma-azumma*, like death had torn his father away.

Eomma-Azumma, more insistent this time, brought his face close to hers. "Shang Ik, look at me, my child." She lifted his head with her hand and caressed his face gently. "This is not forever, my boy. This is just for a moment. All of life is but a passage of moments. This moment too will pass. And we will be together again."

They sat holding hands in the kitchen, attempting to push away the dread of that final moment when they would have to release each other, possibly into an eternity apart.

Escape from Seoul

Don't let them see you. Stay down. Shang Ik crouched down in a farmhouse a few miles outside of Seoul. Hiding in the straw, he held his breath as the sound of marching boots pounded just outside the wooden-planked farmhouse.

Five days earlier, his *eomma-azumma* had sat him down in her kitchen and told him to run away. He had gone to his sister's that night, thinking *Eomma-Azumma* would change her mind the next day. But on his way back to Soon-Ja's home, he stumbled upon an altercation in the middle of the street.

Two men were arguing over the price of a delivery. The first man insisted that the price had not changed, while another businessman refused to pay. The argument escalated, and Shang Ik watched as the man who refused to pay called a policeman whom he seemed to be friends with. Together they accused the first man of being against the communist regime of the North Korean government, and the policeman executed him in the street. Shang Ik watched in horror as the man fell to the ground, dropping the basket of fruit he had refused to hand over. The businessman walked over and calmly picked up the basket.

Shang Ik knew then that his *eomma-azumma* was right. It was no longer safe for them in Seoul. He snuck back into Soon-Ja's home a more somber boy than when he left hours earlier.

The next morning Shang Ik and his sister's family awoke to the North Korean People's Army soldiers taking complete control over the city. Soldiers from the South Korean Army, who had not retreated with the government, were valiantly attempting to hold the line in the city and took to fighting the North Koreans in the street.

All that day Shang Ik and Soon-Ja's family stayed indoors, keeping away from the windows and taking turns keeping the children quiet. Twice that day, they heard a knock on the front door from soldiers. One time, a North Korean soldier demanded information on the whereabouts of the South Korean army. Another time a company of South Korean soldiers banged on the door, demanding to know if any North Korean soldiers had been by the residence. Both times Soon-Ja informed them that they had seen nothing and quickly shut the door.

As the day wore on, Shang Ik became more and more worried about *Eomma-Azumma*. His thoughts went to his *uibus-eomi* as well, but he felt confident that her new husband would keep her safe. *Eomma-Azumma* had no one, and Shang Ik determined that he would wait until nightfall and then sneak out to see her.

As soon as the sun began to set, he crept out of the window in the bedroom he shared with Soon-Ja's young son and darted into the empty streets. He stayed away from the main roads, sneaking around the backs of buildings and houses until he came to her house.

Creeping up to the door, he looked around him nervously and lightly tapped. "*Eomma-Azumma*," he whispered loudly.

There was a movement inside, and he heard her on the other side of the door.

"Shang Ik?" she asked fearfully.

"Yes, *Eomma-Azumma*! Open the door!" He looked around him nervously, not wanting to be discovered.

The door opened, and a hand pulled him inside. *Eomma-Azumma* closed the door behind her and held Shang Ik for a moment in the silence.

"*Eomma*, soldiers are everywhere. What if they come for you?"

She pulled him away from her and held his shoulders firmly. "Shang Ik, you have to get out! You must leave here tonight." She walked over to the corner and produced a pack with some clothing and food that she had prepared for him. "Don't worry about me. I will be just fine here. I will stay hidden. No one will come for me. But you are young. You are what they are looking for to join their army. You cannot stay here. They will either try to recruit you or kill you. They don't want you growing up to be a soldier who can fight against their communist regime. There is no more time. You have to go tonight!"

She pulled out an old map from inside her apron, detailing the general South Korean territory. She began hurriedly to give Shang Ik some basic instructions, showing him on the map what cities he should expect to find along his journey.

"You put the rising sun to your left, and you just keep moving. Don't stop for anything."

Shang Ik tried to listen, but he was certain that the rushed lesson in geography would stick with him.

"You go to sleep now, Shang Ik. Rest for a few hours, and when it gets darker, you will leave."

Shang Ik spent the remainder of that evening lying on a cot in the corner of the room, waiting for nightfall to arrive. His mind raced. Over and over he reviewed the map and the contents of the pack his *eomma-azumma* had prepared: extra socks, two shirts, several apples, and some dry bread. He tried to remember the route she showed him, but his thoughts kept shooting off in different directions. *How will I know which village to stop in? Will Soon-Ja worry and try to find me? How long will that food last? I could eat all that in one sitting! What should I do if I see a soldier? Should I hide or try to hit him? Maybe only if I hit him from behind.*

"Shang Ik, wake up now. It's time to eat before you leave."

Eomma-Azumma shook awake Shang Ik, and he obediently got up and came to the table. He hadn't rested a bit, but it didn't matter now. He and *Eomma-Azumma* ate a meal together in silence, the pack she prepared for him sitting ominously by the door.

After several moments, *Eomma-Azumma* reached into the pocket of her apron and pulled out a gold pocket watch. "Your father and I knew each other long ago. We were good friends. I took this to give to you. I knew after his funeral that sometimes people take things just to pay for bills. They mean no harm, but I knew he would want you to have it. It's yours now, Shang Ik. Keep it."

She placed the watch on the table quietly and quickly went to stand by the window. Shang Ik stayed seated, staring at the watch he hadn't seen for months. He hadn't bothered to look for it because he had avoided any tangible acknowledgements of *Appa*'s passing. But there it sat. Small but regal, just like he was.

His father's pocket watch struck 11:00 p.m. *Eomma-Azumma* quietly walked over to the doorway, pausing for a moment. And then without a word, he bent to pick up the pack. Shang Ik stood up and came over to her, allowing her to secure the pack onto his narrow shoulders.

Eomma-Azumma kept averting her eyes, focusing on adjusting and then readjusting his pack. She peeked out the window one more time, but the darkness told her that all her neighbors were already asleep. Shang Ik stared at the ground and then lifted his head to plead with her one last time.

"*Eomma*, you can come with me. It won't take you long to gather your things. We should leave together. I shouldn't leave you behind."

She shook her head and smiled sadly, pulling him close and holding him tightly. "Shang Ik, I would slow you down. There is nothing else we can do. You have to go now." Her tears fell freely as she held the boy, heartbroken.

She clung to him desperately as if there were something in their hug that could redeem the time she felt she had lost. "Go, my child," she whispered. "Go now. Don't stop until the sun begins to break in the sky. Then find somewhere to hide until the sun sets again. Go!"

She pushed him out the door, and Shang Ik ran, crisscrossing the road to stay in the shadows, not stopping until he reached the city limits. Once there, he turned to look back at the city, so big and beautiful. It had once been a haven for him.

He knew that, once he left the city, he would likely never see his family again. It took every ounce of strength he had to pull himself away and turn down the road that took him away from the city of Seoul.

~

After Shang Ik's departure, *Eomma-Azumma* closed the door, leaning against it for strength before finally collapsing in tears. She stayed that way most of the night. The next day she tried to go about her business as best as she could. But thoughts of Shang Ik traveling at night alone, possibly being caught by North Korean soldiers, robbed her of sleep.

The next evening she sat in her kitchen, boiling hot water for tea, when she dropped her last remaining teacup at the sound of pounding on the door. She quickly stood and then looked around her to make sure that nothing incriminating was laying out in the open. Brushing her hands on her apron, she opened the door.

A bayonet pushed through the doorway, pointing directly at her face. "Are you Chang-Nyo?" The North Korean soldier holding the gun demanded sternly.

Trembling, she held her hands at her throat. The sight of more soldiers filling the little room caused her to freeze in fear. Another soldier yanked her arm away from her chest, and she cried out in pain.

"Are you Chang-Nyo, former associate of Chun-Soo Moon? Answer me!" the first soldier commanded as he lifted his hand and smacked her across the face.

She fell to the ground trembling and spitting blood. "Yes…I am."

The soldier who slapped her reached over and lifted her by her arm. "You have been accused of conspiring against the North Korean government. Chun-Soo Moon was a South Korean government worker; therefore, you are guilty of treason. You will be executed. Take her away."

She was still reeling from shock as two more soldiers pinned her arms behind her back and pushed her out the door. She barely had time to register what was happening. As she was led out her front yard and down the main road, she saw some of her neighbors peeking out their windows with looks of terror across their faces.

She passed the corner market where Shang Ik and Seung-ik used to spend so much time, where he would sometimes buy sweets to bring to her when he visited in the afternoons. The sight of the familiar store brought Shang Ik to her mind, and she began to panic.

Her cry of agony sent nosy onlookers running to hide as she kicked and fought like a trapped animal. She screamed a cry of despair from the pit of her soul as she was dragged away from her home, away from her friends and neighbors, and away from any hope of seeing her loved ones again.

The soldiers easily restrained her and led her to an area where the North Koreans had set up a base of sorts. A freshly dug ditch stood at the center of their base, and several men and women stood in a line directly in front of the ditch with their hands tied behind their backs. They were pleading for their lives as soldiers lined them up.

Chang-Nyo was dragged to the end of the line and made to stand next to a man who kept falling to his knees and pleading. One hit to his head with the butt of a soldier's rifle stopped him from dropping to his knees anymore.

She stood there with her hands tied, her eyes darting around the base. Soldiers were nonchalantly standing before them, examining their rifles and ignoring the screams from their prisoners. One soldier stood apart, his arms crossed in front of him, his face unmoving.

Chang-Nyo peered closer at him, and her heart stopped. It was Mr. Lee, Chun-Soo's old friend. She would often see them together around Seoul. He had even stopped by her house once when he was walking home with Chun-Soo and Shang Ik. She tried desperately to make eye contact with him, but he turned away.

The commanding officer stood in front of the soldiers, and all stood at attention. The prisoners grew silent to see what the man would say to their now silent guards.

"Before you men are several traitors to our new government. Many of them worked for the former government; some helped hide traitors. Killing those who commit such high treason will bring great honor to the North Korean People's Army and to our communist comrades."

He turned to the group of prisoners and nodded his approval. Pointing to Chang-Nyo, he extended his arm. "This woman was closely associated with a high-ranking member of the former government. She deserves to die a traitor's death."

The soldiers cheered, and Mr. Lee joined in, clapping as he approached the commander.

"I knew this woman, Commander. She and her associate were certainly traitors. Allow me to be the one to bring this honor."

Chang-Nyo watched in horror as the commander nodded and clapped Mr. Lee on the back, handing him a rifle. She shook her head. Her desperation caused her voice to come out in a high-pitched shriek. "Mr. Lee! No! Please do not do this! We were good to you! We—"

Mr. Lee's slap across her face silenced her. He had reached her in three strides of his long legs and put all his force behind his swing. As she crumbled to the ground, he leaned over and picked her up, forcibly attempting to stand her upright. After a moment, he turned and marched back to the line of soldiers. She stood with her hands behind her back, trembling as tears flowed down her face.

The commanding officer lifted his arm and gave the command. "Ready!"

"Please. Please don't do this," Chang-Nyo pleaded as the soldiers made ready with their weapons.

"Aim!"

Mr. Lee expertly aimed his rifle squarely at Chang-Nyo's chest.

"Fire!"

~

Shang Ik walked for hours that night until the sun began to peek over the horizon. He collapsed that first day under a shady tree at the edge of an open field. He hid during the day, observing anxious movements of people everywhere he went. Although he was farther south than Seoul, the rumors of the fall of the city of Seoul spread throughout all of South Korea. From time to time, he would stumble upon families packing up their belongings and preparing to move even farther south.

Not long after he began his journey, a farmhand hoeing a patch of land saw him wandering down the road and called out to him for help. "Hey, you! Boy! Come over here and help me pull this root out!"

Shang Ik hesitated, not sure if he should ignore the man or stop to help him.

"Come on, boy! I need help with this. Come help me. I don't bite."

Shang Ik came forward. He reached out to grab the root, and the man stopped him.

"No, you put all your weight on this shovel here, and I will yank up the root. Ready? Together now. Pull!"

Shang Ik laid all his weight onto the shovel that acted as leverage while the man pulled the root out of the ground. After several minutes of effort, both collapsed onto the dirt, with smiles of satisfaction on their red faces.

"Good work, boy. Thank you."

Shang Ik nodded and stood up, ready to leave.

"Hey, are you looking for some work? I need some help around here. My boss wants me to harvest everything we can before the North Koreans reach us."

Shang Ik stiffened at the mention of the North Koreans.

"If you want, I'll talk to the boss, and you can help me get this job done. He'll give you a little something, and you can be on your way. What do you think?"

"Well, I…I'm not sure. I don't know."

"What's wrong, boy? You have too much money?" The man laughed boisterously at his own joke.

Maybe I should just take it. I can use the money to keep traveling. The food Eomma gave me is almost running out. It will only be for a little while, and then I'll move on.

The man slapped Shang Ik hard on the shoulder, causing the boy to flinch. "Well? What do you say? Shall I go talk to the boss?"

"Yes." Shang Ik nodded. "Thank you. I will help you."

The man went into the home to make the arrangements. They agreed that Shang Ik would work for the man for the next week at least, and he could sleep in the barn. For three days, Shang Ik worked at this farmhouse, helping with harvesting their small crops and feeding what little animals they had.

One afternoon a few days later, after a particularly rough time out in the field, Shang Ik came into the barn adjacent to the farmhouse for a drink of water at the pump. He pumped the lever three times, filling his tin cup with water. He took a few large gulps and then threw his head back and emptied the rest of the tin over his face.

Sunlight shone through the wooden siding of the barn, and the water droplets hanging from Shang Ik's hair and face picked up the light like jeweled beads. As he stood quietly trying to cool off, he heard a strange sound from far off. It was a steady, low rhythm getting louder and louder, as if it were moving closer. He set down the tin cup and moved over to the window to see what it was.

He peered out the window. Then he threw himself onto the ground and crawled over to a pile of hay in the corner, burying himself under the straw. *Soldiers!*

Through the slats in the side, he could see a company of North Korean People's Army soldiers marching past the farmhouse. Their boots hit the ground in perfect unison. Rifles were slung over their right shoulders, while their left arms swayed to the beat of the march.

Shang Ik's heart beat faster as he tried to stay still under the straw. Eventually the entire company passed the barn and made their way down the road. Shang Ik stayed still until they were out of sight. Then he stayed in the hay for another twenty minutes, by his own estimation. After a long while, he crawled out, sneaking out of the barn and into the farmhouse. The farmhand was already at the door, waving him urgently inside. Shang Ik ran in, and they shut the door behind him.

The farmhand and Shang Ik sat on the floor where their employer was, all of them trying desperately not to be seen by the soldiers.

"Did you see that? The North Koreans are here!" The farmhand shook his head in disbelief.

His boss spoke in a frantic whisper. "Well, of course they are here, you fool! What did you think we've been preparing for? We've been hearing rumors about the invasion, and nobody believed them. Now look. They're here!" The boss shook his head with anger. "Those communists are going to come after everyone now."

Shang Ik straightened a little at that.

"What do you mean, boss? Come after who?" Shang Ik exclaimed desperately.

The boss spoke in a loud whisper, with urgency peppering his speech. "Don't you know there are communists already here in South Korea? They've been waiting and hiding for the North Koreans to come, and now they're going to try to get in good with them. I was in Seoul early this morning getting supplies, and I heard that some have already started turning in their neighbors. A bunch of communist sympathizers came out of the woodwork, turning on anyone they thought the North Korean soldiers would be interested in. Mostly government workers and their families, but still—"

Shang Ik jumped up desperately. "Who? Who did they turn in to the North Koreans?"

"Shhhh! Sit down!" The boss hissed. He and the farmhand clawed at the boy, trying to get him to crouch down.

He pulled away from their grasps. "Who did they turn in? Can you tell me any of their names?"

"I don't know who! I simply heard that many people have already been arrested who had once worked for the government. Even members of their families were being arrested. The North Koreans have already begun to occupy Seoul. They're rounding up anyone whom they think is a threat to them. Hey! Where are you going?"

Shang Ik did not allow his boss to finish his sentence. He bolted from the door and left little tufts of dust from the pounding of his feet on the dirt road.

Triumphant Return

Shang Ik ran as fast and as long as he could, stopping only until his legs gave way. He collapsed beneath a tree, hiding there until daybreak. The chirping of a bird jolted him from his sleep the next morning. He rose, momentarily disoriented, but facing the rising sun, he stretched out his hands and followed his left arm north toward Seoul.

He stopped several times that day in villages to get some water and to ask for food. Everyone he spoke to warned him that he should be running away from Seoul, not toward it. He could only give those kind people thanks for their concern, but he had no intention of heeding them. He needed to reach Seoul. He needed to know what had happened to his *eomma-azumma*.

He reached the city by nightfall and was bombarded with the sights and sounds of chaos. North Korean soldiers were still patrolling the streets. Shang Ik crept in the shadows and behind buildings, avoiding the main road. He stayed hidden, trying to make his way to his sister's house without being seen.

As he walked, he could sense the change in the atmosphere around him. The few people who were out and about at this time had looks of terror on their faces. They walked nervously, hiding themselves from being noticed by soldiers or policemen, all of whom seemed to be North Korean sympathizers.

There was smoke from some buildings that had been set on fire as demonstrations of deterrent against anti-communist sentiment. Many buildings also had bullet holes in them from when North Korean and South Korean soldiers brought the fighting to the streets of Seoul.

Shang Ik crept through back alleys, trying to remain hidden. Sneaking through empty buildings and deserted side roads, he finally made his way to Soon-Ja's house. He tapped on the door lightly, hoping not to attract any attention. Down the road, he could hear soldiers patrolling the area. He tapped again, more urgently.

The door opened a slight crack, and his sister's small voice quietly asked, "Who is it?"

"It's me, Shang Ik!" the boy whispered loudly.

The door opened wider. Soon-Ja grabbed him by the shirtfront and pulled him inside. "Shang Ik! What are you doing here? Where have you been?" She hissed through her teeth as she locked the door with her baby daughter in her arms. She gasped when she saw her brother's dirty and haggard appearance.

"Where did you go? Where have you been? We've been worried about you!"

"Where is *Eomma-Azumma*? I heard that the North Koreans were capturing everyone who used to work for the government as well as their families. *Eomma-Azumma* was afraid they would come for her. What has happened to her?"

Soon-Ja nervously jostled her baby in her arms as she looked down at the floor. Shaking her head, she walked over to the baby's bassinet and set her down. Then she turned to her brother with outstretched arms. "Shang Ik, come sit with me."

Shang Ik hesitated by the doorway. "Is she safe? Is she OK?"

Tears were already filling Soon-Ja's eyes. "Shang Ik, just come with me. Let's sit down."

The heightened emotion and fear that had driven Shang Ik to run back to Seoul spilled out from him in that moment. "No!" he yelled, pulling away from his sister.

Soon-Ja turned to him and began to plead with him. "Shang Ik, we tried to stop it. We sent word for her to come here and hide, but it was too late. A neighbor or someone turned her in to the North Koreans."

Shang Ik stood trembling, his face a deep crimson, shaking his head in denial. "No! No! No!"

"I am so sorry, Brother. By the time the news reached us, they had ordered her to be executed by firing squad." His sister broke down in tears as she gave him the news.

Shang Ik turned and ran out the door. He ran down the road, out into the streets, this time not caring who saw him. He ran until he reached that shady hillside where he and

Seung-ik had first heard the cannons days earlier.

He ran, climbing to the top of the steepest hill there. When he reached the top, his knees buckled, and his shoulders collapsed as he plummeted to the ground. He prostrated himself, his face on the ground, his tears creating a puddle of mud. This was a nightmare. This had to be another nightmare. *It's a dream, Shang Ik. Just wake up. It's just another dream.*

But with each breath of dirt he inhaled, he was still awake. He was still here in this hellish and twisted version of reality, where his father was dead, his stepmother had abandoned him, and the only other mother he had known was dead. He was all alone. He was living the nightmares that had so long haunted his sleep. The river was cascading around him, and this time there was no bottom. Night was falling. There in the dirt, he wept.

~

He must have passed out because he awoke hours later to a stray dog licking his face and the sunlight peeking over the horizon. The dog licked at his tears and the tracks of mud and dirt that were on his face. Then the dog barked and trotted off down the hill. Shang Ik sat up, feeling completely numb. He remembered reading the newspaper with his father years ago, when they would tell stories of soldiers coming home from fighting in the Second World War. Many were suffering from a condition that the articles described as shell shock.

He knew now what that meant because he was shocked to his very core. *Was it possible that just recently his father had hugged him goodbye and left him by the school building?* It seemed like only this morning he and *Uibus-Eomi* had prepared breakfast together while they laughed and told jokes, and surely it was just a few days ago that he giggled as *Eomma-Azumma* measured him for a new suit while she jokingly scolded him for fidgeting. Now they were all gone.

He stood to his feet, his knees still shaky and unsteady. Seoul stood before him, dark and broken. It was no longer the beacon of refuge and safety it had once been for him. Now it was an adequate representation of how he felt, a ruptured shell of its former self. He trudged down the hill toward his sister's home, utterly uncertain of what would become of him.

His sister did not scold him for leaving or staying out all night. When he walked into the home red-faced and dirty, she simply gave him sympathetic looks as she handed him clothing and wash towels to clean himself.

Soon-Ja's mother-in-law was not so accommodating. "This boy is a bad omen. Since he showed up, all the chaos and destruction that came upon our city happened. He has bad energy, and now my son may be dead!"

The old woman would often interrupt her daily ritual of bowing to one lifeless figure or another, loudly bemoaning Shang Ik's presence in her home. Shang Ik spent most of his time avoiding her constant criticism and trying to ignore her hurtful accusations.

Now the city of Seoul was completely under North Korean rule. The summer months went by quickly, and once fall came, North Korea occupied almost all of South Korea, except for a small portion of the southeast corner of the Korean Peninsula.

As the weather began to cool and September came around, there were rumblings of the small and much weaker South Korean army making headway against the North Koreans. No one in Seoul could openly spread this news for fear of retaliation, but whispers were spreading throughout Seoul of how an American military force led by General McArthur was landing the invasion force at Incheon Harbor and giving aid to the South Korean army.

It was late August, and now people in Seoul were hearing how the North Korean People's Army hurled everything in its arsenal at the US infantry divisions. The US Air Force stopped the North Koreans at the Naktong River, and by the second week of September, the North Korean army had utterly exhausted its reserves, losing most of its tanks and artillery.

By September 15, the American and South Korean armies had destroyed nearly every military target in North Korea. On September 29, President Syngman Rhee returned to Seoul and reestablished the government of the Republic of Korea. Led by General McArthur, Seoul was at last liberated from North Korean occupation.

The news of Seoul's liberation was met with only momentary joy, overshadowed completely by the rejoicing at the return of Jong-Pil from the south side of the Han River. His homecoming was met with tears of joy from his relieved wife, shouts from his small children, and exclamations of rapture and idol worship by his emotionally unhinged mother.

The South Koreans met those few months of liberation from the communist regime with rejoicing. Shang Ik enjoyed the freedom to go outside, no longer afraid of the North Korean military. He even visited some of his old school friends.

After the South Korean government regained authority in Seoul under the leadership of President Syngman Rhee, the weakened government wanted to establish pockets of authority throughout South Korea now that the North Koreans had been forced out. Many police and government officials were assigned to establish leadership throughout the South.

As police section chief, Jong-Pil was first in line to be assigned to another location. The South Korean government ordered him to govern south of the Han River. Unfortunately his homecoming was short-lived, as he was soon forced to leave his wife, two small children, mother, and young brother-in-law behind again.

His mother was particularly incensed. "Why do you have to go? You did you not tell me you would have to leave! Have them send someone else!" The old woman railed at her son while she sat rocking in her chair, crying, cursing, and yelling.

Jong-Pil tried to remain calm. "There are already rumors of the North Koreans pushing back against the Americans and our military. Other rumors say the Chinese are about to come to the aid of the North. We have to quickly establish ourselves as an independent South Korean government. They need leaders to govern in the areas that the North Koreans destroyed or left abandoned during their retreat. This is my duty. I must go."

His mother shook her head as she rocked back and forth, continuing to wail. Jong-Pil turned to address Soon-Ja. "I am just going south of the Han River. If you believe for any reason that the North Koreans will return to retake Seoul, take the children and go to our ancestral home in Mang-Ri. It's just south of Suwon. I have a homestead there, and my elder brother and some of the relatives live there. You should be safe."

Soon-Ja simply nodded her head, trying to suppress her tears as she rocked her baby in her arms.

Jong-Pil put his hand on her shoulder for comfort and then turned to look at Shang Ik.

"Shang Ik, I want you to be as helpful as you can here in the house. Help your sister with the children and try to stay out of trouble. Be aware that, even though we are free now, our situation can change in an instant. Be vigilant. Now say goodbye to me, brother." Jong-Pil extended his hand for Shang Ik to shake.

Shang Ik stood tall and began to walk over to Jong-Pil. He was about to shake his extended hand when the old woman's claws nearly yanked his arm out of its socket.

"It is all your fault this is happening, you stupid little pig! You brought a bad omen to this house! My son has to leave because of you!"

She raised her hand as if to slap him, but Jong-Pil pulled him out of her grasp and shoved him out of the room. The old woman collapsed into a fit of tears and began frantically bowing to one of the tiny statues she had scattered about her home. Shang Ik could hear Jong-Pil scolding his mother from the other room where he sat, hiding from her vitriol. He shook his head. *Now I'm going to be stuck here with her for who knows how long.*

With Jong-Pil gone again, Shang Ik stayed busy helping Soon-Ja with everything he could. He took on more chores and made it his business to stay out of the old woman's way.

General McArthur's campaign to invade North Korea all the way to the northern border of China had been successful, giving the slightest glimmer of hope that the end of the war was imminent. This hope was short-lived.

Radio reports that November gave the distressing news that three hundred thousand Chinese army troops crossed into Korea as reinforcements for the depleted North Korean army. With the help of the Chinese, the North Korean army regained much of the ground they had lost, and the American and South Korean militaries suffered many defeats. They began to retreat, and word spread that once again the city of Seoul was in danger of falling to the North Koreans.

As winter came, the threat of a North Korean takeover of Seoul became more serious. People built makeshift bridges and pontoons to cross over the river that led them farther south. As the time passed and they received no word from Jong-Pil, Soon-Ja feared he was dead. She sadly began to make arrangements for her family to travel to her husband's ancestral home in Mang-Ri.

It took a few months to find someone who was willing to take the small family, including two children and some possessions, on a dangerous journey. Eventually she was able to hire a guide who was willing to take their group, although they had to go on a cart driven by cows.

Soon-Ja tried to convince her mother-in-law to accompany them, but she refused to join them. Shang Ik was secretly relieved.

Soon-Ja tried to convince her. "*Eomeonim*, if we don't leave now, we won't get another chance. When the war first came, they took Seoul in only three days. We've been hearing for a while now that the North Koreans are gaining traction and that the Americans and South Koreans are retreating. The North Koreans are coming back, and we need to take advantage of this warning we've received and leave now."

The old woman shook her head. "I won't be leaving. This is my home. My son will come back for me. He will come back." Then she gestured rudely to Shang Ik. "I won't take another step with this bad omen you brought into this house!"

Soon-Ja stepped forward and spoke firmly with tears in her eyes. "I don't know what has happened to my husband. He may be dead. I have to do what he told us to do. At least if he has survived, he'll know where to find us. You do what you please. But my children and I are leaving."

The old woman irrationally covered her ears. She would hear none of it. She sat in the doorway, weeping for her son and muttering prayers to every empty deity she could find scattered about the small home. Shang Ik watched with sadness at her desperate attempts to find solace in tiny figures made of wood or stone. For the first time since he had come to this unwelcoming house, Shang Ik felt sorry for her.

It was now winter. Shang Ik, Soon-Ja, and her two small children packed up everything they could carry and began their march with a small group of people traveling farther south as refugees. The group traveled for several days. Shang Ik mostly walked while Soon-Ja and her two children sat in the cart pulled by the cows. Everywhere they went, there were rumors of McArthur's army losing more ground and being pushed farther south. Now they had to fear not only the North Koreans but also the Chinese.

As they traveled, they heard stories of a sea of men, a great number of Chinese soldiers who were causing the American military to retreat, gaining further territory for the North Koreans. Because of the presence of this Chinese fighting force, US Air Force planes were constantly surveilling the area, dropping bombs meant to annihilate this new Chinese threat.

One evening as the sun began to set, Shang Ik rubbed his neck and asked the man driving their cart, "How much farther to the next town?"

"We are coming now to the town of Uh-Jung-Geh. We will rest there and start again tomorrow."

Someone yelled out from the group as Shang Ik and their guide stood talking. "Quiet! Everybody listen!"

The group stood still as they heard the unmistakable sound of marching boots behind them. Whatever soldiers were in the distance were closing in on them fast.

Shang Ik whispered to his sister, "Maybe it's our soldiers. Maybe it's the Americans."

Soon-Ja shook her head and motioned for him to be quiet while she strained to hear what language the incoming soldiers were shouting in. Everyone in the group was frozen, and then as if in unison, the language being shouted in the distance became recognizable to the entire band of refugees.

"Shang Ik," Soon-Ja whispered frantically, "it's the Chinese!"

Run for Your Lives

Soon-Ja jumped down from the cart and grabbed Shang Ik by the shoulders. "Take the baby and anything else you can carry and run!"

He quickly strapped two bags onto his shoulders and took the baby from her arms. Meanwhile the entire group of refugees had begun to flee, some of them screaming. The man who had been driving their cart jumped out and ran with them.

The cart man urged them on. "Quickly! Uh-Jung-Geh is only a few miles ahead. We can take shelter there. Hurry!"

Soon-Ja secured one pack onto her shoulders and hoisted Duk-Soo onto her hips. She turned to Shang Ik, more determined and firm than he had ever seen her. "Run, Shang Ik! Follow me!"

Brother and sister ran as fast as they could, holding fast the two babies in their arms. The crowd moved quickly and chaotically, hoping to find the town soon. As they maintained their desperate sprint, Shang Ik turned to look behind them, not certain what he was hoping to see.

The sight behind them filled him with dread. They saw hundreds of feet behind them. Through the tree line, a company of Chinese soldiers marched in unison, their rifles in firing position.

Shang Ik turned back around and pumped his legs even harder. "They're coming, Soon-Ja!"

His sister turned to see, and terror filled her face. Ahead of them, the entrance to the village of Uh-Jung-Geh glistened like a beacon. The entire crowd of refugees ran for the village, hoping to escape the Chinese who were quickly overtaking them. As the group of people scrambled into the village like mice running into a hole, they all came to a quick stop, confronted with the overwhelming force of a large company of Chinese soldiers.

Shang Ik and Soon-Ja were the last few to make it to the village. By the time they arrived, their group of refugees was huddled in the center of town, surrounded by Chinese soldiers who had already taken control of Uh-Jung-Geh.

The siblings froze. Shang Ik looked at his sister, not sure of what they should do. She only held her son tighter, her face resigned.

The commander of the Chinese battalion stepped forward as his soldiers motioned for all the refugees to huddle in the center of the town. Shang Ik and Soon-Ja made their way to the center of the huddle. Soon-Ja reached out her hand and touched her baby in Shang

Ik's arms. Then she took Shang Ik by the hand to await their fate.

In almost perfect Korean, the officer addressed the refugees. "Everyone, remain calm! We are not here to harm you!"

The Chinese commander held up his hands and tried to smile reassuringly. "We are not here to bring harm. My soldiers have supplies, some dry food. Come and receive what you need in an orderly fashion!"

The commander motioned to his soldiers, who began to set boxes on the ground and hold out cans of dry food. He gestured for the people to take them. No one moved.

The commander raised his hands again, addressing the crowd more enthusiastically. "Come! We know that there are many of you who are hungry or in need. Take these supplies! We did not come here to hurt innocent people. We all have a side in this war, but that does not mean we lose our humanity. Take what you need!"

One by one, people began to step forward, taking the food that was offered to them. With great hesitation, individuals stretched out their hands to receive help from the enemy. Soldiers eagerly held out food with one hand, keeping their other hands firmly on their weapons.

Shang Ik looked to Soon-Ja and shrugged. She nodded him toward the soldiers. "Go on, Shang Ik. Bring one of everything they offer. We have nothing to lose."

She took the baby from him, and he walked forward slowly. He took what food was offered to him with his eyes down and quickly returned to his sister.

After all the food had been distributed, the commander stepped to the center of the crowd to address everyone once more. "Some of the homes here have been abandoned. You may gather in those homes, several families to a residence. My company and I will move on tomorrow, but you are to stay here. This entire region is currently war territory. Soldiers from both sides are crossing through here, and it will be better for you if you stay."

Soon-Ja cleared her throat. "But, Commander, my brother and I need to take my children farther south, where we have family. That is where we are going."

Several others in the group began to address the commander as well, all hoping to convince him that they needed to leave.

The commander simply shook his head. "Everyone is ordered to stay in this village for the time being. With time, you can move on to your destinations, but for now, it is too dangerous to have this group traveling into a war zone. That is all." The commander walked off, and his soldiers spread out, leaving the refugees in the square.

Shang Ik turned to Soon-Ja. "It's like we're hostages."

She looked at her brother and then down at her children. She took a deep breath. "No, we aren't hostages. You heard him, Shang Ik. We can leave when it's safe. He's right anyway. With the South Koreans and North Koreans and now the Chinese and Americans, we're better off staying in one place until we know it's safe to travel."

Shang Ik shrugged his shoulders. Duk-Soo began to run around, eager to release some energy after sitting in a cart for so long. Shang Ik lunged after him to keep him close.

Soon-Ja squared her shoulders and nodded her head. "We'll have to stay here, Brother. Let's just find a home that's big enough to hold us for now. I'm certain we will be able to move on in a few days."

They made arrangements with a group of about twelve people to stay in one house that had been abandoned. Brother and sister took a small room and quickly split up the cleaning and responsibilities with the twelve other refugees.

Two days later, Shang Ik came into the home, pushing through the crowds of people. He found his sister in the kitchen with the other women. Duk-Soo was playing on the floor, and her baby daughter was sitting in a small bassinet someone had lent them.

Shang Ik came up to his sister and began to speak in a low tone. "Soon-Ja, I heard some of the men say they overheard the Chinese soldiers talking about American airplanes. Before they left yesterday, the Chinese soldiers said that American bomber planes were looking for them in all the villages, and they think they will be flying over us soon. That's why they left."

Soon-Ja looked around at the women and lowered her voice to her brother, trying not to draw attention. Everyone was on edge, and the last thing they needed was a panic.

"I'm sure those planes won't bother us here. They'll be able to see that we are only civilians, not soldiers. To be safe, we'll only go outside during the daytime so they can see clearly that we aren't soldiers, OK?"

A tugging on her dress interrupted her. She looked down to see Duk-Soo, covered in mud from head to toe.

"*Eomma*, I make mess." The boy smiled mischievously.

Shang Ik rolled his eyes.

"Oh, you naughty boy! Look at you. Where did you get all this dirt?" Soon-Ja scolded her son.

Then she playfully whacked his bottom and wagged her finger in his face as she scolded him. She stripped him of his clothes and threw them into her basket. She left her little boy in his undergarments while she gathered the basket in her arms.

"You stay with them, Shang Ik. I need to wash these." She picked up the basket and then stopped to put her hand on her brother's face. "And try not to worry. We'll be all right." She playfully took his face in her hands.

He smiled and then pulled away. He crouched down to coo at the baby in her bassinet, holding the mischievous Duk-Soo by the hand to make sure he didn't get into any more trouble.

Soon-Ja exited the house, basket in hand. She made her way toward the outskirts of the town, traveling down a pathway bordered by persimmon trees. The valley was serene as the young woman carried her little basket of clothing toward the stream to wash. She paused when she heard her little Duk-Soo's laughter in the home and smiled to herself while she kept walking. She could just imagine him getting into some sort of mischief while Shang Ik tried to corral him. She could picture Duk-Soo running in his bare feet around the home while her baby daughter slept in her little bassinet.

The sounds of her children and brother faded gently into the wind with the swallow's song as she approached a stream they used for washing and bathing. Soon-Ja set her basket down, tucking her long, jet-black hair into a plain brown headscarf. She reached into the basket she had set on the smooth river stones, carefully removing one item of clothing after another.

Beginning first with her baby's soft cream-colored nightdress, she submerged it into the frigid water quickly. She entered a rhythmic pattern of scrubbing the clothing on the smooth river rocks, dunking one article at a time into the water, wringing dry, scrubbing and pounding again, dunking, and then wringing dry one last time.

Soon-Ja worked quickly, periodically stopping to breathe on her hands and shake off the winter cold. So focused was she on her task that the cadence of her pounding and wringing and the splashing of the water as she dunked and scrubbed that it drowned out the humming sound at first.

But when she stopped to drape a nightshirt onto the charcoal gray rocks to dry, she heard it—a distant yet distinct buzzing sound. She was about to shrug it off and return to her laundry when the noise became louder, pulling her away from her chore. She drew her hands to her eyes and turned her face to toward the sky as she slowly stood to her feet. With her hands shielding her eyes from the vibrant rays of the sun, she made a squinted attempt to distinguish the image on the horizon.

The figure in the sky took shape, drawing all color from Soon-Ja's ruddy cheeks and a hallowed gasp from lips that no longer shivered with the cold.

In the air, the fighter plane quickly descended into the valley at breakneck speed. The young pilot in the craft craned his neck from inside the cockpit of his B-26 Invader. He hopelessly tried to clean the foggy window with his gloved hand as he peered and squinted at the ground below.

He had been on this reconnaissance trip for days, flying over villages to see if he spotted any North Koreans or Chinese. It was hard enough to differentiate the North Koreans from the South Koreans without adding the Chinese to the mix. How did his lieutenant expect him to know who was who from the air?

Grunting, he tipped his wings from left to right, trying to get a better angle of the figure at the water below him. All he saw from above was violent thrusting movements on the rocks below. His heart raced. He knew he had to make a decision fast. *What are they digging into the ground? What if they are trying to bury weapons? Or a bomb?*

Pursing his lips, he shook his head, unsure. He had to risk it. He hadn't seen anything suspicious for days, but they had reports that the Chinese had infiltrated these villages. If they were anywhere near here, he had to take that chance.

At the sight of the wings tipping from left to right as the aircraft made a clear descent, Soon-Ja immediately abandoned her wash and turned with a desperate sprint toward the village, where her children were. The pilot watched as the figure below began to sprint toward the village and craned his neck as far as he could in an attempt to clearly identify the person. *Is that a man or a woman? What was he digging in the ground? Why is he running?*

The pilot couldn't verify the identity of the fleeing figure from that distance. If he waited to confirm his identity, the person might alert soldiers in the village of his presence. If he had a high-powered rifle, he might shoot him down. He had only a few split seconds to determine what he should do.

The pilot watched as the figure below began to sprint toward the village. He tightened his grip on the yoke of the aircraft and then lifted his radio using his call sign to signal his commander.

"I have a possible tally making a beeline toward the village. How should I proceed?"

He heard a few moments of static on the other end as the plane hovered ominously behind the woman while the pilot waited for confirmation on how to proceed. The radio crackled to life after a moment with a single phrase.

"Pilot, you are clear to engage."

The pilot took a deep breath and then positioned his aircraft directly behind Soon-Ja's fleeing figure. He moved his hand off the radio and onto the lever that lowered his high-powered machine gun from the nozzle of the plane.

By this time, Soon-Ja was in hysterics, waving her hands and screaming like a banshee. "Shang Ik! Duk-Soo! Run! Everyone, run!"

The deafening sound of the engine of the B-26 drowned out her terrified plea. The boom of the machine gun was more like cannon fire as the bullets chased Soon-Ja into the town.

They found their target in the courtyard just outside the tiny mud and straw cottage. Plants, shrubbery, soil, and chips of wood and stone exploded into the air. Shang Ik grabbed Duk-Soo and fell to the ground, covering the boy underneath him. Everyone in the home instinctively fell to the ground with screams.

He had heard his sister coming into the main gate in the middle of the courtyard, but the cannonball sounds of the machine gun drowned out any other noise. The walls were immediately shredded to pieces, and sharp glass covered every surface. There were screams of despair, and then there was silence.

The hum of the aircraft faded into the distance, taking with it all hope of life as those who survived kept their faces to the ground, terrified of what they would find when they raised their heads.

A Boy Becomes a Man

Red-hued dust settled to the ground as the sound of the plane grew faint in the distance. At the deafening pulse of the machine gun, Shang Ik had grabbed little Duk-Soo and fallen to the ground as the bullets ripped into the small home. When the noise finally subsided, he slowly raised his head and saw the sunlight shimmering on the shards of glass scattered over the floor.

Immediately Duk-Soo began to cry. Shang Ik slowly put his hands on the ground to steady himself. He winced at the sharp pain he instantly felt in his palms and knees, where pieces of glass had penetrated his skin. He squinted his eyes, attempting to adjust his vision to the distortion of sights and smells around him. The room was ripped to shreds. The thin walls had massive holes, and bullets had riddled the tables and chairs.

He stood, gingerly stepping through the glass, and hurried over to the bassinet. His baby niece stared up at him, wild-eyed but unharmed. He carefully picked the glass off her blanket and lifted her up.

His heartbeat was like a gong in his chest as he surveyed the wreckage around him. He felt the conflict of an internal push and pull. A strong impulse was screaming at him to stay put. Terror and uncertainty settled over him like a weighted blanket. *Someone will come find you. Someone will come for you. Just stay put.*

Another instinct, one that grew stronger with each passing second, instinctively pulled him, beckoning him. *There is no one else. No one is coming for you. You're the one who has to decide. You have to go out and decide what to do. It's up to you.*

While he rocked Soon-Ja's baby in his arms and tried to encourage himself to step outside, Shang Ik had tried not to focus on the ground. The people who had lived with them, those who had traveled that perilous journey with them and coexisted these past couple of days as a pseudo family, had fallen to the ground at the explosion of bullets. The shooting had sent their bodies crashing to the floor, and there they would remain.

Shang Ik forced himself not to stare at their dead bodies. He carried the baby over to where Duk-Soo still stood. The little boy was unmoving, except for his tiny chest heaving in quiet sobs. Shang Ik took his little nephew by the hand and led him through the home, carefully guiding him to step over the bodies that lay prostrate in pools of their own blood.

Shang Ik kept his eyes fixed on the door as sunlight streamed through the bullet holes in the wood. Upon reaching the doorway that led to the courtyard, he stopped. He pushed Duk-Soo behind him.

Squatting down to his level, he looked his crying nephew in the eyes. "Duk-Soo, you stay here. Sit quietly in this corner and don't move until I tell you. You hold the baby, like a good boy."

Duk-Soo nodded and obediently sat with his legs crossed. Shang Ik placed the baby in her brother's arms, facing them away from the door so neither of them would be able to see what was in the courtyard. Shang Ik stood on shaky knees and pushed open the door. The sight before him immediately caused him to double over.

His sister's body was practically unrecognizable. Shang Ik vomited, unable to contain himself. The pungent smell of blood and flesh assaulted his senses, and he could no longer keep his nausea at bay. He bent over, trying to breathe through his mouth when he wasn't vomiting. He wiped tears from his eyes as he struggled to catch his breath. His chest heaved violently; his convulsions caused sharp pains in his side. He forced himself to look up again, and as he stared, his sister's lifeless eyes were the only parts of her not completely shattered.

Shang Ik slowly closed his eyes as he collapsed onto the ground. His head lowered as the tears flowed quietly. *Oh, Soon-Ja, Soon-Ja. What will I do now? What will I do without you? How will I go on by myself? Why wasn't it me? Why couldn't it have just been me?*

Instantly he remembered his sister's children. *What will I do? How can I care for them by myself?* He wiped his mouth with the inside of his shirt and his tears with the back of his hand. He leaned against the doorway, trying to steady his breathing and control the thoughts that were threatening to drive him to insanity. As the chaos of thoughts, sights, and smells swirled around inside of him, the shrill cry of an infant snapped him into focus.

He ran back inside to his niece and nephew. In the corner sat Duk-Soo, still tightly clutching the screaming baby. *What do I say to him? What do I tell him?*

By this time, many people had run into the home, screaming at the sight of so many dead. Many just stood and cried, weeping over the bodies. Some were strangers; others were friends. But all felt connected by the journey they had taken and the circumstances in which they found themselves. Everyone mourned as if he or she were grieving a loved one. Few had ever experienced anything so tragic.

The men began to carry the bodies outside, to prepare them for burial. The women dried their eyes and started to clean and dress the bodies, and everyone gathered together to comfort and provide the little they had for those whose loved ones had been in that house.

Shang Ik sat outside for a long while as Duk-Soo leaned against him, crying for his *eomma*. The baby, mercifully, had stopped screaming. Shang Ik knew that would soon change when she became hungry. He stood holding the children for a long time, thinking through his situation, trying to be anything else but numb and empty.

A woman offered to care for the children while Shang Ik helped the men with burial preparations. The traditional burial rituals were forgone for a more generalized funeral. Several days of grave digging and a few ceremonial songs completed the bleak affair.

Once they finally completing the unmarked graves and were preparing to lay his sister to rest, Shang Ik steeled himself to bring Duk-Soo to say goodbye to his mother.

As he entered the home where he was being kept, the little boy immediately stood and ran to Shang Ik.

The woman who was caring for him whispered to Shang Ik, "He has been watching for you out the window all day."

Shang Ik extended his hand to his nephew and walked slowly with him. He led the little boy just outside of the village, where a last patch of wild hibiscus huddled, beautifully untouched by the recent frost. Although Shang Ik knew the pain of losing a mother and father so suddenly and tragically, he could not find the right words to comfort his young nephew. Perhaps it was because he knew the truth. There were no words. There was no comfort. He picked a few of these last flowers and let the boy hold them.

Shang Ik and Duk-Soo walked hand in hand to Soon-Ja's burial site. The sky was gray and hazy, and the chill in the air added to the emptiness of the event. Kneeling in the frozen ground next to the boy, he watched as the child clutched the flowers in his little fist, squeezing them until his knuckles turned red. Then Duk-Soo silently tossed the flowers onto his mother's grave and sat staring at the mound of cold dirt. Shang Ik searched his mind desperately for an answer that would make this easier for Duk-Soo to understand. He remembered *Eomma-Azumma*'s quiet voice as he prepared to run away.

"This is not forever, my boy. This is just for a moment. All of life is but a passage of moments. This moment too will pass. And we will be together again."

He shook his head. She'd been wrong. That separation that was just for a moment stretched out into a lifetime. And they would never be together again. He wouldn't add to Duk-Soo's pain by feeding him lies.

Their solemn walk back to the village was dreadful. The smell of death still fouled the air. The women made feeble attempts at cleaning the wreckage, but nothing washed away the terrible scent. Something about that scene connected to his feelings earlier at Soon-Ja's grave. They had all been wrong. All the adults were wrong.

Appa said there would be no war, but the war came. Uibus-Eomi said she would keep me if she could, but she didn't. Eomma-Azumma said we would be together again and the pain would pass, but it hasn't. Soon-Ja said those planes wouldn't bother us, but they came right to our door!

As he walked, Shang Ik's anger grew. Every step he took past the people who were trying to restore the damage and wash away the carnage cemented in him an anger and a resolve that he had never felt before. *Everyone who promised that life would be good lied to me. If they didn't know for sure, they could have just told me. Then at least I might have been prepared. I couldn't depend on them. I can't depend on anyone anymore.*

Entering the house where they were now sleeping, Shang Ik sat at the table while Duk-Soo absently wandered off into another room, without any of his characteristic mischief or joyful energy. Shang Ik watched as the little boy quietly walked away. The loss of that child's joy and zest for life felt like the greatest tragedy of all. *He'll never be the same. There is nothing I can do for him just sitting here. I have to do something. It's up to me. No one knows what the right thing is. I couldn't believe them even if they said they did.*

Shang Ik shook his head, feeling almost empowered by the realization that he was finally in charge of his own choices. The burden of that responsibility gave him pause, and he knew that this was the time to do right. That was what *Appa* would have wanted. That was what *Appa* would tell him to do.

I have to finish our journey. I have to take the baby to Soon-Ja's husband's family in Mang-

Ri and send someone to come back for Duk-Soo. I have to make sure her children are taken care of before I figure out anything for myself.

For the next few days, Shang Ik prepared himself for the journey to Mang-Ri. He knew nothing about Jong-Pil's homestead, except for the fact that Jong-Pil's brother now had a home there. He was certain that, if he presented himself as Jong-Pil's brother-in-law and showed the man his brother's child, the family would show kindness to him and take him in.

The next few days were spent in preparations for his journey. He gratefully took what meager food was offered to him, although he knew it would not last him long. He arranged with the woman who had agreed to watch the children to care of Duk-Soo until he could send someone for the boy.

One week after he arrived at Uh-Jung-Geh, Shang Ik stood at the entrance of the town with his baby niece strapped to his back. He must have looked comical with his high school cap on his head and a baby on his back. But no one laughed. No one tried to dissuade him from taking a baby on this perilous journey. No one tried to persuade him to stay and wait for help to come. Everyone had his or her own loved ones to concern themselves with. Everyone was taking risks to escape this hellish battlefield all had been entangled in against his or her will.

Shang Ik knelt down before Duk-Soo. The little boy held tightly to his uncle's hand, gripping it with fear, almost as if he knew he was being left behind.

Shang Ik tried to smile. "Duk-Soo, you stay here with Mrs. Han. She will take care of you. I will send someone for you as soon as I can. All right?"

The little boy only lowered his head, his bottom lip quivering.

Shang Ik took his nephew in his arms and held him for a few moments. "Be a good boy," he whispered in his ear. He quickly set the boy down and walked out of the village, his heart broken beyond tears.

Shang Ik knew he couldn't go straight on the military roads, or whatever army happened to be in command in that area would surely capture him. If they found them in the village, they would surely notice him on the main roads.

He made the decision to take small side roads and mountain roads. Proud of himself for making the smart choice, he put no thought into how much more difficult that terrain would make the journey for him. The winter snow made that way more perilous, and he would have to find shelter in the wilderness, a risk in and of itself without adding an infant to the equation.

He left early that morning and reached the first mountainous road by midafternoon. A light snow began to fall, and by the time the sun was setting, a blanket of white powder covered everything around him. The baby breathed small puffs of hot breath onto his neck, and as he surveyed the area around him, he began to panic. *There is no shelter for miles. I can't see any caves or shrubs or anything. How will we make it through the night? She'll freeze to death.*

Shang Ik continued to press forward through the wind that was increasing in strength until he felt his legs give away. His knees buckled, pitching him forward into the snow. Shielding his eyes from the howling wind, he looked up and spotted a tree that the wind had blown over. With a sigh of relief, he pulled himself up and ran toward it. He quickly settled into the base of the trunk, shoveling aside as much snow as he could with his bare hands.

He leaned against it, using its wide, leafy branches to protect himself from the icy chill. Reaching behind him, he unstrapped the baby from his back and put her on his chest inside his shirt, hoping his body heat would keep her warm. His own breath came in short puffs as the cold began to seep into his bones.

He sat that way for hours, waiting for sleep to come over him. As the winds died down and the night took on an eerie silence, Shang Ik sank into the silence around him, feeling a wave of sadness wash over his soul. *I'm all alone now. There is no one for me, except for this little baby.*

When he set out on his journey earlier that day, he had felt empowered in spite of the ache in his heart. He was taking his destiny into his own hands, being the grown-up for once. He was only fourteen, but it felt good to him to call the shots for once. He took the baby and left, feeling almost confident.

But now, alone on the dark, cold mountainside, he did not feel strong. Any confidence he had in the decision he had made had quickly vanished. He began to realize what he truly was, an abandoned child with no one to care for him.

He held the baby tighter against him as two tears rolled down his cheeks. His soul cried these days without any warning or awareness from him. The vastness of the mountainside with its absence of roads, villages, or any signs of life seemed appropriate for the way he felt inside. *Who would know if I died right here on this mountain? Who would care?*

Hours passed as Shang Ik sank deeper into the snow and further into a depression. There was a strange calm to him, as if he were slowly beginning to accept doom as his fate. *Would it be so bad if this were the end for me? There is no one left for me to miss, and certainly no one left would miss me.*

An owl hooted in the trees above him. He tried to sleep, but sleep would not come. Closing his eyes, he allowed memories to flow freely in his mind, recollections he had not indulged in lately because the pain was too difficult to bear. So he avoided them. He avoided feeling sad, missing people. He avoided talking about it or expressing any feelings of remorse or longing.

But tonight on this mountain, when it was totally possible that he would not wake up in the morning, he indulged. He allowed sweet memories to roll around in his mind, bringing their light, happiness, and joy of heart.

Appa hoisted him up as they wrestled in *Halmeoni*'s garden. *Halmeoni* tenderly piled food onto his plate, humming as she tucked him into bed. *Uibus-Eomi* sang songs with him and walked hand in hand with him and

Appa as they strolled through the park. *Eomma-Azumma* set a plate of cookies before him as she listened to him tell about his day, watching him intently as if there were no more important person in the whole world.

"And, lo, I am with you always, even unto the end of the world."

Shang Ik's eyes popped open and he looked around. *What was that?* The world around him was still dark. Only the wind had died down. He looked down at his chest and could see that the baby was sleeping soundly, comforted by the sound of his beating heart.

The phrase he had heard felt familiar and important, but Shang Ik couldn't place it. Shaking his head, he leaned back against the tree trunk and closed his eyes once more. The moment he did, he heard it again.

"And, lo, I am with you always, even unto the end of the world."

This time Shang Ik sat up a little, looking around again. *What was that? Where did it come from?* He tried to search his mind for where he had heard the phrase or what it meant. *Was it something I had heard in school? Maybe a teacher? No. Was it from a book? Maybe. A film I saw with Appa?*

Suddenly the memory snapped back into his subconscious, and he saw the image clearly, as if it were happening right in front of him. He was in the school yard when he saw a group of boys tormenting a younger boy. They were shoving him and calling him names. He resisted and fought back, but Shang Ik could see he was beginning to waver. Shang Ik ran over to the group of boys, who were all younger than he was. Pulling them off the boy in the middle, he scolded them sharply and told them to get lost.

"Don't worry about them. They're all pathetic. What's your name?" Shang Ik picked up the small boy's books and wiped some dirt off his uniform jacket.

The boy slowly unclenched his fists and, with understandable skepticism, took Shang Ik's outstretched hand. "My name is Whan Soo Lee."

Shang Ik shook the boy's hand. "Hello, Whan Soo. I'm Shang Ik Moon. Why were those boys bothering you?"

"Oh, they just don't like my religion."

"What is your religion?" Shang Ik asked absently as he and Whan Soo began to walk back into the schoolhouse.

"I'm a Christian."

Shang Ik paused just short of laughing out loud, not wanting to be rude. Christians were becoming more commonplace, especially in Seoul, but that didn't make them anymore mainstream. Shang Ik himself had often poked fun at them with Seung-ik when they saw some children dressed in stiff, formal clothes for church on Sundays. They would mock, smug in their freedom to play in the park while their parents dragged those children to Sunday service.

He had always thought it was silly for people to sit in a church on a Sunday, and he told his *Appa* as much. *Appa* agreed, and they had laughed as they enjoyed their Sunday together, free of religion.

Appa didn't condone Shang Ik bullying anyone and had taught him to defend others. But that didn't mean Shang Ik didn't share a laugh now and again with Seung-ik when they talked about Christians.

As he walked with Whan Soo back to class, Shang Ik felt guilty about those times he had made fun of people just like him for no reason. Perhaps that guilt led Shang Ik to say yes when Whan Soo invited him to his church that evening.

"Our pastor is going to show an American film! It's by Cecil B. DeMille, the big director from Hollywood! It's called *King of Kings*, and it's all about God's Son and how he died. Want to come see it?"

Shang Ik didn't, but he smiled politely and shrugged his shoulders.

"You'll like it, Shang Ik. We just get together to sing and learn about God. My pastor teaches, and he's really funny and makes it interesting for us kids too."

Shang Ik nodded. "Uh-huh. So how do you think we will do in the soccer game this weekend, Whan Soo?"

They started to get into the details of the game while Shang Ik artfully maneuvered the conversation away from church. He thought he had avoided any further commitments on the subject, until Whan Soo gave him once last shout across the hall before they went into their respective classes.

"Remember, it's tonight at six p.m. sharp, Shang Ik! See you there!"

Shang Ik hurried into his class, red-faced. By the time they left school that afternoon, Whan Soo had approached him three different times to remind him about the service that night. By that point, Shang Ik had no other recourse. He had to go. He went home that day, hoping *Appa* and *Uibus-Eomi* would say he didn't have to go or, better, he wasn't allowed to go. He crossed his fingers, hoping for a moment of parental restriction.

"You made a commitment, Shang Ik. You said you would go, and you're going."

Shang Ik stared at his father in disbelief. *For this he allows me to go out on a school night?*

"I'm sure they are nice people, although they seem strange to us. Just be polite and come home as soon as it's over." *Uibus-Eomi* reassured him as she handed him his jacket and sent him out the door.

Shang Ik arrived at the small church, resigned and moody. He gave a sullen wave to Whan Soo when he came in and sat next to him, resigned. As the evening progressed, his sour mood lifted. The people did seem nice, and the movie was interesting. There was some action and a lot of blood toward the end, which captured his attention.

After the film, a stocky man whom Shang Ik assumed was the pastor stood at the pulpit and read from his Bible. "And, lo, I am with you always, even unto the end of the world. Amen."

Shang Ik left the church that night in better spirits. He waved goodbye to Whan Soo, thanking him for the invite, and jogged home, never thinking of that passage or those words again.

So why do I keep hearing it now in the silence of a snow-covered mountain in the dead of night? Am I that lonely that I'm hearing things? This can't be good.

He heard the phrase again, as if someone were whispering in his ear. Although his mind told him he must be crazy, he did not feel mad. He felt no chaos or confusion. He felt oddly calm and relaxed, which led him to rationalize that he truly was going crazy.

All right, so someone is saying he is with someone. The pastor said that is what that Jesus said after he died, and his powers brought him back to life. I remember that part of the movie. But who is Jesus with? I thought he went back into the sky.

Shang Ik wrapped his arms around his chest, squeezing the baby tight as he rocked himself back and forth to stay warm. *Jesus said He is with us...with me. Or maybe it's just Christian people He's with. That would make sense.* He sighed deeply, surprised at how sad that thought made him feel.

Then another thought occurred him. *Maybe it's not just Christian people. Maybe He is with everyone, and that is why people become Christians and want to follow His ways.* Shang Ik sat up a little straighter at that thought. *So that pastor said that Jesus said He is with me, even to the end of the world.*

Shang Ik's heart immediately fluttered with a surge of emotion at that thought. *With me? Jesus was with me when? At which moment of tragedy I had endured in fourteen years was Jesus with me? If there were somebody with me, maybe I wouldn't have almost drowned in a frozen river or had to sneak across the border. Maybe Appa wouldn't have died and Uibus-Eomi would have been able to keep me. Maybe Eomma-Azumma would still be alive.*

He rolled his neck to release the tension his anger was causing in him. *And what about what happened to Soon-Ja? We were all each other had, and now I'm all alone! How could any of that happen if Jesus were with me?*

Shang Ik sat with that thought for a moment, seething with pain, bitterness, anger, and fear. His heart raced as each picture of tragedy formed in his mind, like a parade of loneliness and loss. However, he couldn't get one word to leave him alone. One single word kept creeping into his self-conscious, interrupting the record he was keeping of how life had wronged him. The word was *always. I am with you…always.*

Suddenly a picture came to Shang Ik's mind. He imagined a gigantic tower of a figure walking beside him as he crossed over the 38th parallel in the dead of night. He envisioned that figure in the room with him and *Uibus-Eomi* as the police officer told him that *Appa* died. He imagined that figure had sat behind him in the mud when he ran off to weep over *Eomma-Azumma*'s death. It ran behind them as he and Soon-Ja fled from the Chinese, each holding a baby.

Shang Ik's imagination of this figure caused a yearning in his heart that he could not quite understand. The yearning felt deep and primal. It felt more real to him than any feeling he had experienced.

He wanted that figure to be real. *I mean, it would certainly be nice to have someone, some God, actually just be there with you. And that maybe one could talk to it and have conversations with it. That would be nice.*

Strange but nice. And maybe it did help you every once in a while, like Superman.

He began to feel tired as he sunk into that thought, allowing the hope of it to lure him to sleep. *Maybe it can be true. Maybe I do have a superhero. And maybe He'll keep me alive until I can figure out who He is. Maybe He is with me now, and I'm not alone, even if it feels like I am.*

A warmth that enveloped him rocked Shang Ik to sleep. The awesome possibility that alone was something he had never been incredibly soothed his heart.

Prisoner of War

The energetic chirping of a bird overhead pulled Shang Ik from his dreams. The sunlight glistened on the snow as he blinked his eyes in the cold morning air. He sat up quickly, looking around him. *I'm alive.*

He quickly peeked into his shirt, and the baby's eyes were blinking awake as she began to smile and coo contentedly. Shang Ik sat there for a moment as it slowly dawned on him that what he was experiencing should be impossible.

How is this possible? We had no shelter last night. We should have frozen to death. His thoughts about the night before were growing fuzzy, and he needed to keep moving. He stood, stretching as best as he could, and wrapped the baby onto his back again. As he rolled his shoulders and tried to get his bearings, he remembered the words his *jageun appa* had spoken to him years ago when he was preparing to be smuggled out of North Korea.

"If you want to know which way is south, in the morning, face where the sun is. Stretch your two hands out. Whichever way your right hand lands is south."

Shang Ik smiled. He looked up at the sun, allowing the rays to warm his face. Then he stretched out his two hands. He moved in the direction indicated by his right hand, picking up the pace in the morning briskness. The sun shining on the hilltops was almost peaceful, and he spent the next few hours traveling up the mountain, making his own path, avoiding any highways. Shang Ik might have enjoyed that journey had he not been so keenly aware of its purpose.

He walked calmly, often transfixed by nature's beauty. High above the clouds, a bird mesmerized him, and he stopped to stare at its majestic flight. It soared toward him, almost regal looking. As he watched entranced, the image in the sky became clearer.

It wasn't a bird. The figure in flight spread out and became six separate figures, flying toward Shang Ik in a *V* formation. Shang Ik lifted his hand, pulling his high school cap higher on his head, squinting, and then freezing in terror. He looked around him desperately, but there was nothing to shield him or the baby. Everything around him was a snowy canvas of white, and he stood out, an easy target.

The six reconnaissance airplanes passed him overhead, and Shang Ik crouched down, covering his ears and holding his breath. He quickly exhaled when he saw one of the planes circling back around until it was directly above him.

Shang Ik's eyes darted everywhere, looking for a place to hide, but his feet stayed firmly planted in the snow. He couldn't move. Fear paralyzed him.

The plane's wings dipped from left to right, as if the pilot were struggling for a better view of the snow beneath him. Shang Ik continued standing. His legs felt like blocks of cement in the snow. The pilot kept circling. The boy turned and looked up, just in time to see the machine gun portal open up in the nozzle of the plane. A long, thin pole slowly extended. He froze and covered his ears.

The earth-shattering boom of the machine gun shook the mountainside and rattled the boy's soul. The echo of the thunderous firing flew through the snow-covered canyon, sending enough bullets to decimate a small army. Shang Ik stood frozen with his eyes closed and his hands over his ears. He knew there was nowhere for him to run. He expected each shot to be the one that ended his life.

Bullets flew past him on every side, whizzing through the air. He could feel their heat as they soared past his face and body, but he could not move. *I'm dead already. I probably just can't feel it yet, but I've already been hit.*

Another round of the same sequence followed while Shang Ik was still standing. The baby had long ago begun to cry, but her wailing was only audible when the plane stopped shooting and rose higher in the sky. Shang Ik slowly opened his eyes and watched the plane circle around, rise higher, and then join the other five reconnaissance planes in the distance.

Shang Ik's hands slowly lowered as they trembled. For a few more minutes, he stood there completely motionless. Just like that, they were gone.

Bullet fragments littered the white mountainside that had been so pristine and untouched just a few moments earlier. After leaving his trembling palms at his side for a few moments, he raised them again, patting himself all over but finding no holes or blood. He reached behind him quickly, unwrapped his baby niece from her swaddle, and checked her entire body. She was screaming at the top of her little lungs, but Shang Ik saw no blood. She had no injuries, except possibly to her eardrums.

He swallowed the lump in his throat while he looked up again at the sky. His heart was still pounding at lightning speed. The plane was really gone. He clutched at his shirt, holding his hand to his chest the way *Uibus-Eomi* used to do to calm him down. Closing his eyes, he worked actively to steady his breathing and slow down his heartbeat. *You're alive. You're all right. You're still here.*

Surrounded by bullets on every side, he looked down at his own hands and body, still intact. He swallowed hard as the adrenaline slowly left his body, completely depleting him of the energy he had felt just moments before. His mind swirled as he turned, his feet finally becoming unstuck. Still clutching the baby tightly to his chest, he moved forward. His feet were heavy in the snow.

After a few moments of heavy trudging, he stopped to again secure the baby onto his back. Continuing his journey, he would reach behind him periodically as he walked to comfort her until she eventually stopped screaming.

Each step he took up that mountain for the next few hours brought crippling anxiety. With every howl of the wind or flap of a bird's wing, he was certain that a reconnaissance plane was going to return to finish the job. Hours later, he wearily stumbled upon a small hamlet tucked into the mountainside.

Once the little village came into view, he stumbled into the town, relieved at the prospect of shelter. The village was tiny, with no more than twenty or thirty houses that he could count. He roamed around, trying to find someone whom he could ask for food. Maybe he could work a few hours in exchange for shelter and supplies. But as he walked the town, it became clear that the village was deserted.

He peeked through windows and snuck into open doors, hoping someone had left behind a few vegetables or some bread. He found nothing edible. One home had some chickens roaming in the yard. He exhausted himself even further trying to catch one, but his pathetic attempts were unsuccessful. He hadn't done much chicken chasing in Seoul.

After a thorough search of every home, Shang Ik walked back to the center of town, feeling dejected. The baby's soft whimpering made him scratch his chin nervously. If she didn't get some milk soon, she would be in trouble. He removed his cap from his head and rubbed his eyes, not sure if the exhaustion he felt were from lack of sleep or if he were weak from hunger.

"Halt!" a deep voice commanded loudly.

His hands dropped from his eyes, and he looked up, staring straight into the barrel of a gun. Shang Ik's hands shot straight into the air as two Korean soldiers ran toward him, weapons raised. One of them moved behind the boy, squaring his rifle directly at the infant strapped to his back. The other soldier reached out and began to search Shang Ik with one hand, his other still on his rifle.

Once satisfied that the boy was carrying no weapons, the soldier stood three inches away from Shang Ik's face and, shouting, began interrogating him. "Who are you? What are you doing here? Where have you come from?"

Shang Ik swallowed the lump in his throat and lowered his hands, his mind racing. *Was this the North Korean People's Army? Or was it the Republic of Korea Army, from the South?* He hadn't learned to distinguish their uniforms, and in their snow gear, Shang Ik couldn't tell the difference. *If I couldn't tell who they were, how would I explain myself? One wrong answer and I'm dead.*

His eyes darted all around him. He began to panic. As he cleared his throat, trying to stall for enough time to formulate an answer, the soldier in front of him lowered his weapon slightly, revealing the mark of the gun was a Carbine. The gun had been well advertised throughout Seoul prior to and leading up to the outbreak of the war and was commonly used by South Korean soldiers. He knew enough of the English alphabet to recognize the letters "USA" on the gun.

USA! The United States is fighting for us. They're South Koreans!

Relieved, he stammered out an explanation. "I am a South Korean refugee. I am running away from Seoul before North Koreans overtake it once more. I am going farther south to Mang-Ri."

The soldier lowered his weapon and grabbed Shang Ik by the elbow. He signaled the rest of his men to retreat, and they all quickly and quietly left the village. The soldier kept his hands on Shang Ik's arm as he dragged him out of the village. Shang Ik tried to keep one eye on the man's rifle while he tripped and struggled to keep up. Desperately, he reached backward to assure himself that the baby was still safely on his back.

The army moved silently over to a small hillside just outside the village. The soldier dragged Shang Ik over to a hollow on the side of the hill and shoved him forward. His foot hit something hard, and he tripped, stumbling onto his hands and knees. Wincing, he stood up quickly and brushed the snow off his pants. He stopped when his eyes caught the sight of a boot on the ground, presumably the same boot that caused him to stumble. He slowly looked around, taking in the sight before him.

On the ground lay about fifty South Korean soldiers. A white tarp covered them, completely camouflaging them in the snow. The soldiers had been crawling up the hillside, elbow by elbow. A radio crackled, and he heard information and instructions being relayed by the soldiers as he was led through their company. The Chinese had advanced farther south, and this reconnaissance team of soldiers was defending the territory. They had been surveilling the very village into which Shang Ik had eagerly walked. He had walked right into the front line of the battle.

The soldier dragged him a good way further from the village. When they finally stopped, Shang Ik was brought to where two other civilians were sitting in a huddle. One was a traveling shoe repairman, who sat with his young son in his lap. Another was a man who had a knapsack filled with pots and pans. Several soldiers had their weapons trained on both men, while another soldier was in the middle, interrogating them.

"I will only ask one more time. Did you see any communists in that town?"

Both men shook their heads emphatically, pleading for their lives. The repairman raised both hands before him.

"No, sir! Like this man said before, we both arrived at the village last night and saw no one!"

Shang Ik was pushed to the ground next to the men. He raised his arms as theirs were.

The interrogating officer turned his attention to Shang Ik, who sat up straight, ready to tell the truth that he also had not seen any communists in that village. But the soldier only looked at Shang Ik. Then he turned and walked away. Shang Ik slowly lowered his hands, and the other civilians did the same.

From a location a few miles away from the outskirts of the village, the soldiers had been scouting the small town, undetected. The captain of that company of soldiers stood silently surveilling the town, a few feet from where Shang Ik sat with the civilian prisoners.

The captain turned to another officer. "Lieutenant! Tell me if you can see anything just over that ridge."

The lieutenant took the binoculars from the captain and peered through them, silently. "Captain, I believe something is moving in the tree line to the right of the village. About a hundred yards out."

The captain nodded in agreement and motioned for a soldier with a large weapon to come stand beside him. The young soldier jumped up from the ground and immediately stood at attention before the captain.

"Fire that bazooka in the direction the lieutenant indicates."

"Yes, Captain!"

The soldier hoisted the bazooka and squared his shoulders, ready to aim.

"Ready!"

The lieutenant kept his sight on the target as he looked through the binoculars.

"Aim!"

Shang Ik pulled the baby from his back to his chest and covered her ears.

"Fire!"

Upon the explosion of the bazooka onto its target, the tree line lit up with enemy gunfire. What they thought had been an empty village became a fireworks show of enemy artillery. The South Koreans threw off their white tarp with a shout and opened fire on the North Koreans. Shang Ik crouched low to the ground with the baby in his arms, covering her with his body.

Bullets flew through the air as the South Koreans tried to hold their ground. Men began to fall to the ground as the North Koreans returned fire and began to advance on the small group. The captain seemed intent on holding the line until twenty minutes into the battle when his lieutenant ran to him, holding his shoulder, which a bullet had grazed.

"Captain! They are closing in, and we will soon be overtaken. We are greatly outnumbered. You must signal the retreat!"

The captain looked at his wounded lieutenant and then at the rest of his men. Many of them lay bleeding on the ground, while a few brave ones were valiantly shooting at the enemy, trying to hold the line.

He took a deep breath and shouted at the top of his lungs, "Retreat!"

Every soldier still standing turned and ran as the North Koreans pursued them. The captain ran to the civilians under his charge at the top of the hill. Shang Ik held the baby in his arms as he trembled, waiting for instructions from the captain.

"You have two choices! Stay here or come with us! If you come with us, you had better keep up."

"And if we choose to stay and hide?" the repairman asked.

The captain unstrapped his sidearm from its holster. "You will be shot! We will risk nothing being given to the enemy!"

Shang Ik looked at the other two men, who simply nodded at the captain and gathered their things. It was too late to secure the baby onto his back again, so he carried her in his arms as he struggled to keep up. Shang Ik and the other civilians were red-faced and short of breath as they brought up the rear of the retreating company of soldiers.

They ran as best they could, stumbling and gasping for breath, at the tail end of the group. On the run, the captain ordered a radio request for help to a nearby air force base. Shang Ik paused for a moment to catch his breath. His side winced in sharp pain.

The moment he did, the captain turned and aimed his gun directly at the boy. "Are you coming or not? Decide!"

Shang Ik immediately picked up the pace, grabbing at his side with one hand as he ran. After twenty minutes of running, F-86 fighter-bombers from the American air force base flew overhead.

For the first time, the sight of an American military plane brought relief to Shang Ik, as the fighter-bombers opened fire on the pursuing enemy. It took the surviving South Koreans another fifteen minutes to reach the hilltop, where they met with reinforcements.

Mercifully, the captain ordered them to stop and rest. He received radio confirmation that the communist soldiers and the entire village were demolished. Shang Ik's chest contracted heavily as he sucked in large gulps of air. He held his niece tightly in his arms while she screamed of terror and hunger.

The soldiers who survived the onslaught lay in the woods, while their compatriots from the other battalion gave them water and medical attention. It was then that the captain turned his gaze fiercely to Shang Ik and the other civilians who were with him. Shang Ik was still trying to catch his breath, and he sat holding his side as he took deep breaths of air.

The captain stormed to the civilians and ordered his soldiers to seize them. Shang Ik opened his mouth to protest but stayed silent when the soldiers came and violently lifted the other prisoners but left him alone.

The men and the little boy with them screamed their protests. The little boy cried as he screamed.

"*Appa! Appa!*"

Shang Ik's heart ached at the sound of the boy crying for his father.

"Detain those men! Throw them on the ground now!"

The soldiers violently grabbed the two men and shoved them into the snow, while one yanked the little boy out of his father's arms.

"*Appa!*"

The little boy screamed for his father at the top of his lungs while a soldier kept the man to the ground with his boot on his back. The other man began talking as fast as we could.

"I swear I know nothing! I don't know what this man saw, but I saw nothing!"

The captain approached them swiftly, a revolver in his hand. He began his interrogation. "So! You said there were no communists in that village. Isn't that what you said?"

"Honestly, we did not see anyone in the village!" both men asserted in concert.

The captain aimed his revolver at the traveling repairman.

"No, please! You have my word!"

The captain ignored him.

"These men are communist spies! They will be executed for their crimes!"

The soldiers immediately lifted the two men off the ground and began to drag them toward the woods, followed by another soldier holding tightly to the screaming boy.

Shang Ik covered the baby's face with his hand and closed his eyes as three deafening shots silenced their screams. For a brief moment, there was silence.

Shang Ik kept his eyes closed until he felt a poke at his chest. He slowly peeled his eyelids open to reveal a soldier pointing the barrel of his rifle directly at his chest. Shang Ik recoiled and held the baby closer.

"This boy must be a spy as well. Tell me, boy. Are you a spy?"

"No, sir!" Shang Ik cried, shaking his head vigorously. The soldier shouldered his weapon and ripped the baby out of Shang Ik's arms as she screamed. Shang Ik lunged for her, but before he could protest, several soldiers pounced on him, beating him and punching him. One soldier took a wooden stick and began to hit him repeatedly.

"Confess! Confess your crime! Tell us who you are!"

The captain and lieutenant supervised this ordeal for a few minutes before finally ordering them to stop. When they did, Shang Ik lay on the ground, barely able to move. Every breath he took caused sharp pain in his side and face, and his eyes were bruised and bloody. The captain walked over the blood-covered snow and shoved the boy with his boot. Shang Ik looked up at him out of one swollen eye.

"You saw what happened to them." He pointed in the direction the three bodies were dragged.

"Now talk."

Shang Ik tried to sit up on his knees, wiping the blood from his mouth. "Captain, I am a refugee from Seoul. My sister and I left Seoul with her two children. My parents are dead. My sister is now dead. That baby is her child, my niece. I am trying to take her to her family in Mang-Ri. I was hoping I could live with them. That is all. That is why I am here."

The captain watched him. His stoic face showed no signs of approval or disapproval.

The lieutenant shook his head. "I don't believe him, Captain. What is a young boy doing alone in this kind of area? I bet the communists sent him here, and they gave him the baby as a cover to get across without suspicion."

Shang Ik shook his head, weak from pain. The captain and lieutenant walked away and conferred with another officer. Shang Ik looked around and found his niece in the arms of a soldier, who was jostling her gently to keep her quiet. Shang Ik was desperate to keep her in his sights. The captain sent the officer to Shang Ik, and he recognized the man as the same officer who had been interrogating the other men earlier that day.

The soldier wasted no time in trying to get a confession out of the bleeding boy. "What is your name?"

"Shang Ik Moon."

"What high school did you go to?"

"I attended Whi-Moon High School in Seoul."

The soldier scoffed with disbelief. "Oh, is that so? I happened to also go to that high school. Tell me about the school."

Shang Ik desperately searched his mind for memories of his school days. They seemed so long ago.

The soldier prodded. "Tell me. What about Professor Cheung? Is he still there?"

Shang Ik felt a wave of relief. "Yes, he is. Old Cabbage Head is still there."

The soldier's countenance changed at the familiar nickname of the teacher. He began to laugh. "Old Cabbage Head! That is right!"

The chuckling of the soldier momentarily eased the boy's fear. He too began to lightly chuckle.

The soldier reached out and grasped the boy's shoulder. "You're OK, kid."

Shang Ik breathed a sigh of relief.

"Are you hungry? Here, have some of my lunch."

The gnawing in his stomach reminded Shang Ik that he hadn't eaten in a couple of days, and he gratefully accepted the food offered him. The soldier went over to confer with the captain and lieutenant, while Shang Ik intently watched. The soldier gestured to Shang Ik, and the captain nodded and walked away. Shang Ik exhaled slowly.

The soldier returned to Shang Ik. "OK, boy. Now that we know the truth about who you are, what do you say you help us out? How about you spy for us?"

Shang Ik stopped chewing.

"You could go back to the North and report to us about what you find. What do you say? Are you willing to fight for your country?"

Shang Ik lowered the food and swallowed. *If I say yes, I will have to go into communist territory. I will have to fight. I may have to kill. Or someone may kill me. And what will be the point, after I've survived so much, to die this way?*

He shook his head and looked at the officer. "I am sorry, sir. I cannot. The baby needs food. She needs help. I have to take her to her family, or she won't survive."

The soldier looked up to the baby, who was still screaming miserably. The poor infant had been left in her blanket on someone's coat after the men had been unsuccessful in stopping her crying.

The soldier shook his head. "All right. You're free to go."

Shang Ik quickly stood, thanking the soldier profusely. He ran to the baby and picked her up, and his familiar scent momentarily calmed her. He carefully wrapped her onto his back and hurried away from their campsite, away from the soldiers and away from the death that still hung in the air. He ran quickly, not looking back, lest the fate that had claimed the lives of three innocent people and several soldiers came to claim him too.

A Servant or a Slave?

A better part of the day passed before Shang Ik sighted the village of Mang-Ri through weary eyes. Rice patties, covered in winter frost, lined mountain slopes on three sides of the village. Stilted vegetable gardens gave evidence of bleak winter weather. Small single-story homes made of mud and brick with tiled roofs were cloistered in the center of the village, while the outskirts of the town told a different story. The houses away from the center were more modest. They were wooden huts with thatched roofs, scattered about the surrounding fields.

As Shang Ik approached the town, a farmer pushing a handcart filled with dried rice eyed him with suspicion. Shang Ik struggled to stay on his feet, his hands shaking from hunger. The fatigue of starvation threatened to knock him to the ground. His sister had given him only a rudimentary description of the home before the tragedy at Uh-Jung-Geh—a brick home with a small garden in the center of the village. Shang Ik lurched forward, dragging his feet. The baby cried, but her cries were getting weaker and weaker.

He saw the words *KIM* etched into a wooden plank above the door of a modest-size home. Shang Ik sighed, weary and hoping he had reached Jong-Pil's brother's home. He raised his trembling hand to the door and knocked, hoping the baby's cries would send concerned adults to the door and lift the burden off his shoulders.

The door opened, and the woman who met him quickly slammed it in disgust, thinking him nothing other than a dirty transient boy. Shang Ik stepped back and then knocked again, this time more urgently. He was ignored. He leaned on the doorway, desperate. He then quickly unwrapped the baby from his back, holding her in his arms, facing her directly toward the doorway.

With one hand, he pounded on the door. "Please! Mrs. Kim! I am the brother-in-law of Jong-Pil Kim! He was my sister's husband. I came to bring his child to you."

He paused to listen. There was no response. He banged on the door more urgently.

"Please, Mrs. Kim. Please, Mr. Kim! I am Jong-Pil's brother-in-law! I have brought your niece to you. Her mother, my sister, is dead! The baby has no one to care for her. Please!"

He kept banging until the door swung open. A stern-faced man stood in the doorway. Shang Ik took a step backward. Then he jostled the baby in his arms.

"Mr. Kim, I came to bring you your niece. We left Seoul with my sister to bring your brother's children to you. But my sister has died. Airplane bullets killed her almost two weeks ago. She was shot down."

The man showed no emotion on his face, not a flicker of remorse or sympathy for the boy or the screaming baby.

Shang Ik continued, running his sentences together now, eager to plead his case. "Please, Mr. Kim, let me stay here with the baby. I can work for you and help you. But please take her."

The man shook his head, exasperated, and then motioned for Shang Ik to enter. Shang Ik entered quickly, carrying the baby into the kitchen area. He lowered his eyes to the floor as he walked in, immediately aware of his dirty appearance in contrast to the well-kept little room and haughty hostess.

The woman of the house turned her nose up at Shang Ik and began to scold and berate him. "This child is not our responsibility!

Who are you to bring her here? There are six of us living in this house as it is."

Mr. Kim entered and stood next to his wife. The two of them stood over the boy and baby. The man's eyes were narrow, his face red, and his fists clenched. The woman seemed ready to pounce at any moment.

A hiss came from the man's mouth. "My brother chose to live and work in Seoul. I inherited this home. What makes you think that child is entitled to anything I have?"

"Look at her!" his wife interrupted. "She is skin and bones! And who is going to put up with that screaming? I won't take her! She is your responsibility." At that, the woman left the room with a stomp, muttering and complaining under her breath the entire way.

Mr. Kim stood, stoic and unfazed. Shang Ik had been staring at the ground as they scolded him for bringing a dying baby to their care, a dying baby who was their blood relative. He was dirty. He was weak with hunger and fatigue, and he had no other options.

Swallowing his pride, Shang Ik raised his eyes to call to this uncaring man. "Mr. Kim, I will take care of the baby. Only please allow us to stay here. We've come a long way. And we have nowhere else to go. I am strong. I can work for you."

Mr. Kim sighed and pursed his lips. His brow was knit in thought. After a minute, he rolled his eyes. Curtly he responded, "Most of the servants have run off. I could use extra help. Besides, she is my brother's child. You can stay and work for us. But the baby is your responsibility."

Shang Ik lowered his head in thanks. Mr. Kim came close to him and wagged his finger in Shang Ik's face. "Remember, boy, you have to care for this child. You may work for us and earn your food and hers. But this baby is your total responsibility." With that, Mr. Kim turned and left the room.

The baby's cries faded away slowly as her hunger gave way to exhaustion. Alone in the kitchen, Shang Ik stayed, staring at the ground. The numbness set into his chest as he held the baby, blankly staring at the floor while he gently rocked her in his arms. *Just survive. There is nothing here for you or out there. Just survive. Just for today and then one more day. Just survive.*

The baby's thin face was drawn and pale. She had become quiet now and whimpered in her sleep. His stomach growled, reminding him of his last meal two days ago. He sighed. They were both starving. *At least we'll have some food. That's something.*

The lone remaining servant came out and motioned for Shang Ik to follow him. He set the boy up in his quarters, a mat on the floor. Shang Ik lay the baby on the mat, and she immediately began crying. The servant shrugged his shoulders, not having anything to offer a screaming infant.

Shang Ik crept into the kitchen and poured some rice in a small bowl. He ran outside and pumped water into the bowl, smashing the rice with a spoon. Coming back to the mat, he squatted on the ground and tried to spoon-feed the rice water to the baby. She eagerly took some, but then her screaming continued until she exhausted herself and fell silent. Nothing he could offer would satisfy her intense hunger.

Shang Ik lay down next to the baby, not eager to leave her and begin working the next morning. He kept the little bowl of rice water by his side in case the baby woke up. Although he was physically exhausted, Shang Ik couldn't sleep. He lay there with his hand on his chest and the baby by his side, staring at the straw-thatched roof while waiting for dawn.

It was sunrise, and the servant shook the boy awake. "Wake up! You have to go collect firewood before the morning breakfast."

Shang Ik sat up, rubbing the sleep from his eyes, surprised he had been able to sleep for a few moments at least. He turned sharply to check the baby, but for the moment, she was sleeping. He sighed with gratitude.

The servant continued to urge him. "Get up, lazy! Go to the mountains and cut enough firewood for the day. I have to begin my chores."

Shang Ik crept from the house as everyone else slept and went on a solitary hike up the mountainside. Mang-Ri was a sleepy little village, peaceful and serene. He allowed himself to feel the morning breeze and be momentarily comforted by its coolness. A sharp pain in his foot from the forest's brambles brought him back to his reality. He had no shoes.

Attempting to cut firewood in bare feet was a painful affair. After he cut all that he could carry, he stumbled and struggled down the mountainside, wincing in pain with almost every step.

When he finally entered the home and began to stack the wood in the kitchen, a young boy came out of the bedroom, stumbling with sleep. He was about Shang Ik's age. Shang Ik stopped stacking the wood when the boy came out, and the boy stopped rubbing his sleepy eyes when he noticed Shang Ik. They stared at each other.

Shang Ik thought of the hour and a half he had just spent in hard labor, leaving him already dirty and tired although the day had just begun. This boy had slept in and would be able to enjoy being served his breakfast. The boy stared at Shang Ik with mild curiosity. Then he sauntered over to the table to wait for his breakfast, never lifting a finger to offer to help Shang Ik or the other servant.

Shang Ik, angry now, lowered his head to hide the redness of his face. As he continued stacking the wood, he noticed the stains and blisters in his hands. In that moment, the baby let out a cry, giving him the excuse he needed to leave the room in a hurry.

Shang Ik fed the baby some more rice water, which she took with tears and moans. He attempted to silence her and rock her back to sleep. When she finally drifted off, Shang Ik peeked around the corner and saw the family gathering around the breakfast table. He backed away and then went outside. At the water pump, he pumped furiously into his hands and scrubbed the dirt off his face and neck. The water was ice-cold, adding to the chill of the early morning mountain air. He pumped some more until he was satisfied that he was no longer dirty or disheveled. He shook his hands and head to get the water off and then came to join the rest of the family for breakfast.

He entered, and most were already sitting down, as Mrs. Kim served them their meal. Shang Ik came to sit at the end of their table, where there was an empty space.

Mrs. Kim looked up with a start. "What do you think you are doing? You do not sit here. You sit over there with the other servant."

If Shang Ik closed his eyes, he swore he could hear Soon-Ja's mother-in-law. The two women were cut from the same cloth. The lady of the house then pointed at the other side of the room, where a small table stood isolated. Shang Ik looked around at the family, who were all staring at him, waiting for him to get up. Quietly he moved over to the other table and sat, swallowing the lump in his throat.

He could smell their delicious breakfast of white rice with meat and vegetable soup. The thought of having such a satisfying meal tempered the embarrassment and shame building up inside him. When the lady of the house brought their breakfast to the table, the sight of a meager bowl of barley and broth, with no meat and only little vegetables, dashed Shang Ik's hopes.

He stared at the bowl, willing himself not to shed any more tears. He looked up and caught the eye of the other boy, who seemed to wait until Shang Ik was looking and then shoved a large spoonful of hearty meat and vegetables into his mouth. Shang Ik's eyes drifted back to his own plate.

"Oh, it seems Mr. Moon is not very hungry this morning," the lady of the house sarcastically stated, knowing full well the boy had to be starving. She piled more food onto her son's plate.

Shang Ik continued to stare at the small bowl of thin broth and could not bring himself to take a bite in spite of his hunger. "Yes, ma'am. I am not so hungry this morning."

He set down his spoon and excused himself. Entering the room where the baby slept, he gingerly lay down on the mat, trying not to wake her. He stared at the ceiling again. The lump in his throat made it hard for him to breathe. He roughly wiped the tears that escaped the sides of his eyes, but they were coming uncontrollably now, and he could not contain them. Turning over on his side, he covered his mouth to muffle the sound of his sobs.

The next few months were a lesson for Shang Ik in growing accustomed to hard physical labor and emotional neglect. When Shang Ik was not cutting firewood for the meals or helping the servant and Mr. Kim around the house, he was taking care of his niece.

Because she was too young to eat real meals and there was no milk for her, all she could eat was rice with water. She would cry as she ate and would wake up every night several times to cry. Each time, Shang Ik would rouse himself and spoon-feed her more rice water until she could cry no longer. As the months went by, Shang Ik spent more time fussing over her. She was becoming skin and bones, and his pleas to Mrs. Kim for help were constantly rebuffed.

Nearly three months after they arrived at Mang-Ri, Shang Ik opened his eyes one morning after a particularly peaceful night's sleep. This night, the baby's crying had not disturbed his sleep. He lay in bed a minute or two, enjoying the uninterrupted silence. Rubbing his eyes, he almost smiled at how refreshed he felt. The silence had been golden. *The...silence?*

Sitting up quickly, he turned to touch the baby, but she was cold. He rushed to uncover her blankets, lifting her chest to his ear. He heard nothing. He held her in his arms, staring at her intently while trying to see her chest lifting or any flicker of movement. He held her, and tears sprung to his eyes, dropping onto her lifeless body. He rocked back and forth. A moan escaped his lips as he pulled her into him, hugging her little frame tightly as he wept. He wept uncontrollably, sobbing and groaning, holding her tightly in his arms as if trying to squeeze life out of her.

An hour later, he emerged. Her tiny figure in his arms had been wrapped in a blanket. The servant had informed Mr. and Mrs. Kim of the baby's death, and they stood in the kitchen, waiting for Shang Ik.

As he entered, Mrs. Kim stood quickly from her seat. "So she has passed?" she asked with a soft tone, not quite caring but without its usual bite.

Her husband poured himself tea and calmly addressed the boy. "Her burial is your responsibility, Shang Ik. Make sure you take care of it before you begin your evening chores."

Shang Ik was surprised that he felt no more pain at their words. He only stared, allowing his anger to show. Slowly he left the house, marching into the garden. Angrily he grabbed a shovel with one hand and walked out of the village, up the eastern hillside.

Winter was just ending, and the ground was still mostly frozen. Shang Ik set the baby's body on the ground and began digging. He dug for what felt like hours, not caring to report back to the house anytime soon. When the blisters in his hands told him he could dig no longer, he threw the shovel on the ground and sat. It was still a shallow grave despite his efforts, but it didn't matter. Nothing mattered to him anymore.

He set the baby gently into the grave. *I should have gotten a flower.* Reaching into his pockets for anything to memorialize her, he pulled out some lint, dirt, and the small wooden spoon he had been feeding her with. He kept it in his pocket to hide it from Mrs. Kim. He turned the spoon over in his hands for a moment and then crouched over and laid the little spoon on her chest.

After filling the grave with dirt and snow, he sat back on the mountain, observing the village beneath him. From his perch on the shallow grave, everything was serene and peaceful, a stark contrast to the turmoil he felt in his heart. *What should I do now? I came here for her. Now where will I go?*

The sun rising higher in the sky reminded him that Mr. Kim was waiting. *I'll stay here for now and work for them. At least I'll have some food. I have nowhere else to go.* He turned to take one last look at the grave, resolving to never again return. He just didn't think he could bear it.

Shang Ik continued to work for the family into the spring and summer months. As the season changed from winter to spring, the entire village began work in the rice patties. Shang Ik had never worked in a rice patty before this, but he learned quickly that it was arduous and exhausting work. In the mornings, he would gather firewood. He was barefoot most days. When he stepped on a stone or twig and stumbled down the hillside, he would enter the home dirty and bleeding, sometimes limping.

"Oh, these city boys are good for nothing," Mrs. Kim would say. "They don't know how to work."

Shang Ik would ignore her and run out to the garden to wash himself at the pump. Eventually it became pointless to wash himself because he was just going to be submerged in muddy water from the rice patties all day. He would walk out of the muddy water after a long day of work in the rice patties, completely covered in leeches.

A year came and went as Shang Ik worked for the family. In the spring and summer, they harvested rice. In the fall and winter, they worked around the home. The following spring, Shang Ik stumbled home after a long day in the rice patties. Every day was a struggle between hunger and exhaustion. Most nights, exhaustion won. One particular night, he collapsed onto the mat and slept undisturbed until morning.

His eyelids fluttered open at the warmth of the sun peeking through the window. Still groggy, Shang Ik licked his cracked lips and rubbed his eyes. He yawned and stretched like a house cat, hoping to catch at least a few more minutes of sleep. Lifting his head, he strained to listen for Mr. Kim or the other servant. As he did, he noticed a slight pulling sensation on his leg.

He sat up and threw his thin covering off his leg. Then he flinched strongly in disgust. A leech had been sucking the blood from his calf all night and had grown to almost three times its size. Wincing, Shang Ik gently leaned over and tried to poke at the object hanging like a vampire bat off his leg. Immediately it popped, making the sound of a corkscrew coming out of a bottle, sending splatters of blood onto Shang Ik's hands and face.

"Ugh!"

The boy jumped off the mat and ran outside to the water pump, violently scrubbing his hands and face. Frustrated, he stopped pumping and bolted from the village. He ran down the main road up the mountainside. He kept climbing, dragging himself up through the brambles, using his hands to pull himself forward. When he finally reached the top of the mountain, he looked around and let out an intense, gut-wrenching scream.

"Aaaaaaaaaaaaahhhhhhh!"

His chest heaved as he sucked in the cold, thin mountain air. Some birds flew from their nests, frightened by the scream. His knees buckled underneath him as he sank to the ground. Tired, he looked for the village from there. It was, as always, more peaceful from far away.

Shang Ik looked up from where he sat, trying to find a higher perch. *There is no point in going on like this. I just need to end it. End it right here. No one will care. But at least it will be over.*

He turned his head quietly, measuring the mountainside, but couldn't find a cliff from his vantage point that would be more fatal than painful. He wondered if he could stay on the mountain and not move. He could just let himself starve slowly. *I wonder how long that would take. Maybe a few days.*

He rolled his head back and lay in the grass, contemplative. After a few moments, he sat upon his elbows, one thing certain in his mind. *I know one thing. I'm not going back to that house.*

The thought of entering that home again made him nauseous. He lay back on the grass for a few minutes, feeling trapped. If he got up, he would have to return to that hellhole. If he stayed, maybe he could gather the courage to end it all. He propped himself up on his elbows, peering past Mang-Ri, toward other smaller villages. Their similar small-town feel gave him no respite, and he wondered what was beyond this cluster of villages. The thought hadn't fully entered his mind when he sat up and crooked his neck.

Looking around him, he scratched his head. *Why do I have to go back at all? Why is it either death or that house? Why not just go somewhere else? I've heard Mr. Kim talk about Suwon, a town not far from here. I remember he was angry because the Americans had built a military base there.*

He stood tall, trying to crane his neck to see as far past the villages as he could, wondering what was out there. *Well, anything is better than what I have here.*

He patted his pocket. The three thousand won he earned from his year and a half of working were still there, in the secret lining he had sown into the pocket.

He nodded his head. His heart was racing. *That's it. I'm leaving. I don't know why I wasn't killed all those other times if I were just meant to die here in this awful place. And if I stay here, I might as well be dead.* His heart told him there was something more he had to do, some obscure purpose for his life, but it was too deep a mystery for a boy who had just turned sixteen.

He stood quickly. The quiet little town seemed even farther away now, and he was glad of it. Hurrying, he stumbled down the mountain, pushing back leaves and skipping over the brambles in a rush of excitement. The memories of his past survival emboldened him. He squared his shoulders as he walked, lifting his head taller. *I've survived much worse than this. I can do this. Maybe someone else couldn't, but I can.*

He reached the road and started a sprint, leaving the village and all the pain associated with it behind.

An Orphan in Suwon

Shang Ik guarded his three thousand won like he was protecting precious metals. It wouldn't buy much. It only amounted to about three US dollars. But Shang Ik was hesitant to dip into his payment for a year and half's worth of labor. He kept it in its secret location, a resource of last resort. He needed to find work quickly.

He found Suwon easily enough. It was one of the larger cities south of Seoul. Shang Ik was having trouble finding some way to pay for food. He regretted his decision almost immediately when he entered the city and found he had nowhere to stay and nothing to eat.

He wandered about the city his first day there, naïvely expecting to come upon some job right away. In his sixteen years, he had been hungry, and he had struggled, but he always had a plan. He generally knew where he was going next and what he needed from the people around him. Now his future was entirely up to him.

Shang Ik wandered aimlessly, approaching businesses and marketplaces and asking for work. "Excuse me. I'm looking for work. Are you looking to hire someone?"

Most would shake their heads and continue their work. Others would rudely flick their hands at him as if to shoo him away.

"Excuse me. Do you have any work?"

"Not now. Go away, boy."

He was dismissed, ignored, and sometimes pushed aside. He hurried down the main road and found a modest home. While he knocked on the door, he tugged at his shirt to make himself presentable. A young woman opened the door.

"Hello. I just arrived in Suwon. I have nowhere to stay. Can I sleep in your shed in exchange for work?"

The young woman meekly shook her head and closed the door. He left, searching for another home that might look welcoming. After several more rejections, he knocked on more humble cottages or small apartments, even shacks. All refused to give him shelter for the night.

As the sun began to set, the boy started to give up hope of finding a job or a place to stay that day. The clang of metal gates slamming shut and windows being closed announced that men and women were packing up their wares, closing down their shops, and heading to their homes. Soon the city square was almost deserted.

Shang Ik leaned against a building, his arms folded and his head bowed. A passerby might think he was relaxing, but a heart was beating quickly underneath the folded arms. *What am I going to do now? I've got to find some shelter soon.*

As the sun began to set and twilight covered the city, a loud flapping sound interrupted Shang Ik's panic. He looked around the corner from the building he had supported himself on. Above the main doors of the city hall, a large white canopy was stretched out. Its flaps were blowing with the gentle breeze. *Oh well. At least I won't get wet if it rains.*

He ran toward the city hall and found himself a secluded corner. Leaning with his back against the wall of the building, the moonlight streaming in through the white tarp, Shang Ik settled in as hunger gnawed at his stomach. *It's only one night. Tomorrow I'll find work and someplace to stay.*

Shang Ik's optimism was short-lived. He spent the better part of the following day going door to door, begging for food, shelter, and work. No one would help him. No merchants needed extra help, and no businesses were hiring. All that day Shang Ik sought help, and by the end of the day, he was desperate. The three thousand won remained secreted in his jacket. He was too afraid to spend it, fearing it would be his last meal.

He was walking around town with his shoulders slumped and his head down. He had run out of ideas, and he was contemplating moving on to the next town. Lost in thought, he wasn't paying attention when he plowed into another boy. This one looked a few years younger than he was.

"Watch it!" the boy shouted with annoyance.

Shang Ik looked up and saw several young children in a group, just casually standing together. He took his hands out of his pockets. "I'm sorry. I wasn't watching where I was going."

The boy nodded and sniffed. Then he smiled and held out his hand in a good-natured way. "That's all right. I'm Chin Hwa."

Shang Ik shook the boy's hand. "I'm Shang Ik Moon. What are you all doing here? Don't you go to school?"

The boy laughed, and the others joined in. "No! We don't need to go to school, work, or anything. Nobody tells us what to do."

Shang Ik looked at the boys. They were younger than he was. "But don't your parents mind?"

Chin Hwa frowned, and his countenance darkened. He shuffled his feet in front of him and lowered his gaze. "Don't have any parents. They died in the fighting." He gestured to the other boys. "Their parents are dead too. We're all orphans."

The words stung Shang Ik's heart but also consoled him with the kinship he immediately felt. He straightened his shoulders and lifted his head as if to signify that there was no shame in what he was about to say. "So am I."

Chin Hwa's face brightened, and he smiled, grateful not to have received the rejection their society gave to those who had to beg in the streets.

Shang Ik returned the smile. "Chin Hwa, do you know of anywhere I can find some work? Or some food?"

Chin Hwa shrugged his shoulders and shook his head. "I don't know about work. No one here wants to help us. But there is somewhere you can go. There is an American air force base just outside the city, toward the south. I hear they sometimes give people work."

Shang Ik started to shake his head at the mention of an American military base, but before he could refuse the suggestion, Chin Hwa offered some other advice. "And if you're hungry, follow me!"

He turned and ran. Shang Ik looked around, startled. Then he took off running after the boy. The boys jogged outside the city, down the main road for a mile or two. In the distance, he could see the air force base and wondered if they were going there. But Chin Hwa veered to the right and led him to a large field.

Someone had nailed a makeshift wooden plank onto a tree stump. In a beginning English class at his high school in Seoul, Shang Ik had learned to read simple English words. Written on the plank was the word "DUMP." This was where the American army was disposing of its garbage.

As the boys stood looking onto the field, Shang Ik could see several children already walking around and through the smelly mounds. They carried buckets, old cans, anything at their disposal. He walked closer and saw that the children were scavenging through the garbage, throwing items into the buckets. They collected old chicken bones, crusty bread, half-eaten sandwiches, and apples, emptying anything edible into those buckets.

"We take what we can and boil it in water for soup. That's how we all eat," Chin Hwa said matter-of-factly, as if there were nothing irregular about getting one's food out of a massive, stinking garbage heap.

Shang Ik fingered the few won he had in his pocket and tried to reason with himself. *If I use the money for food now, I'll have nothing. I'd better try to make this work until I'm sure there's no other way.*

All that week Shang Ik ate from the dump with the other children. He would scavenge for scraps of meat and half-eaten fruit and bread and then boil the meat to eat in a stew. Chin Hwa also showed him a tent for refugees of the war set up by the South Korean government. It stood, dismal and crowded, down the road from the air force base.

At night, orphans and people left destitute by the war slept huddled together on the floor of that tent. For a week, Shang Ik spent his days asking for work, his evenings picking through the dump for his food, and his nights sleeping on the floor of a moldy, cold, damp tent.

The second day he was in Suwon, he walked into the Suwon K-13 Air Base with trembling knees and sweaty palms. He did not feel encouraged by Chin Hwa's assertion that the base gave people work "all the time." Still he knew he had to try.

In the distance, B-26 Invaders and North American F-86 Sabre Jets were arranged neatly on the tarmac, their awesome firing power hidden from view. As Shang Ik stared at the alignment of American warplanes, vivid memories flooded his mind of the last time one of these killing machines confronted him.

He felt the chill of the mountain snow from when he stood frozen as the plane attempted to shoot him down. He smelled the stench of blood and flesh at the home at Uh-Jung-Geh. He suddenly felt nauseous, and for a moment, fear threatened to send him running from this terrifying sight. He forced himself to look away from the planes. *They can't hurt me sitting on the ground like that. I'll just try to see if they have any work. I can't be afraid forever.*

Averting his eyes from the heavy weaponry, he wandered around the base until he saw a sign written in Korean that said "Labor Office." The line was already long. Several men and women were also looking for work. Shang Ik took his place at the end of the line and waited his turn.

When he finally reached the window, the woman there began to speak in a tired voice before Shang Ik could even ask a question. "We have no jobs right now, but if you sign your name to this list, you will be considered when a position becomes available." She shoved a clipboard in Shang Ik's direction. He scribbled his name and scurried away when the woman yelled, "Next!"

Leaving the labor office, Shang Ik looked back on the long row of people who had been lined up behind him. He noticed even more coming into the base. He also saw his hope of finding work as an unskilled adolescent diminishing.

Every day for that week, Shang Ik came to the base to check on his status at the labor office. In the evenings he would rummage through the garbage dump or ask for more work in Suwon. Exiting the labor office one day, he was nearly run over by an American soldier, looking straight ahead, whistling as he walked briskly. His dark blue uniform had many colorful patches near the left lapel. As Shang Ik hopped out of the man's way, his uniform and his aura of authority captivated him. *That man looks like an officer. He must be high ranking too. Maybe if I can get help from him, I'll have a chance.*

As he was observing the man, a group of four or five small children ran up to him, crowding around him and asking for money or food. Their little hands clawed at the man's uniform. Their dirty faces and ratty clothes stood out sharply in contrast to the man's sharp blue uniform and jaunty officer's cap. The children's bare feet left dust marks on his highly polished military boots.

The officer paused, taken aback by the many mud-stained hands waving in front of his face. He smiled and held up his hands to calm them. Then he reached into his pocket and gave whatever coins he found to the children before hurrying into the labor office. The small group of vagabonds huddled together, counting the money, before another soldier came out and chased them away.

As they ran past him, Shang Ik recognized many of the children from the dump where he got his food and from the refugee tent where he slept. *I have to be smarter than that. I have to stand out, or they'll never give me a chance. They'll just chase me away like those children.*

Shang Ik turned to leave for the day, deep in thought as to how best to approach the officer about his situation. As he was leaving, though, he noticed another soldier in a blue jacket hurrying past him, holding a piece of paper. He waved down an officer, saluted, and then handed the man the paper. The officer immediately gave the soldier his attention and read the note carefully before the two men walked off together. *A letter! That's what I must do! I must write a letter in English and give it to the officer. That will impress them.*

Shang Ik hurried back to the labor office, asking the young woman there for a piece of paper and a pencil. She shrugged her shoulders and obliged him, and Shang Ik took it. Then he ran off to a shady place and sat to compose his letter.

His English was minimal. He only remembered a few words from his English class in Whi-Moon High School. With great difficulty, he put together a few sentences that he hoped illustrated how difficult his life had been and how much he needed this opportunity. He tried to communicate his desire to study or work. He wanted to impress on these soldiers that he was someone to whom they should give a chance. That's all he wanted, a chance to show what he could do.

He neatly folded the letter and put it in his pocket. *This has to work.*

He made his way back to the labor office area and leaned against a fence that faced the main entrance. About forty-five minutes after he arrived, the same officer, the one who nearly ran him over, the one who had given money to the poor children, emerged. Shang Ik took a deep breath. Then he broke out into a jog toward the man, waving the letter in his hands.

"Sir! Hello, sir. For you!"

The man turned immediately and stopped. He was tall and slim. His sharp jawline outlined a long face. His countenance did not soften when he saw Shang Ik, but he waited patiently for the boy to catch up. As Shang Ik approached, he handed the man the letter with a bow of his head. The officer took the paper with a nod and began to read. His eyes moved back and forth quickly as he skimmed the letter.

The corners of his mouth turned up into a smile. He chuckled lightly. "So you can speak English."

Shang Ik nodded enthusiastically and then thought better of it. "Eh...I no speak good...but I write."

The officer nodded and continued reading. He pursed his lips for a moment and then shifted his gaze, peering down at Shang Ik. "What is your name, young man?"

Shang Ik squared his shoulders and lifted his chin. "I am Shang Ik Moon."

"Well, Moon, let me see." The officer rubbed his chin and furrowed his brow. "A chaplain from America just arrived at the base yesterday. He might be able to use some help. Would you like to work for a chaplain?"

Shang Ik panicked at the question, searching his mind for recollection of that word. *Chaplain? What is a chaplain? I'd better say yes and find out later. I may not have another chance for work.*

Shang Ik quickly bobbed his head up and down in the affirmative. His hair fell before his eyes with the vigorous movement. "Yes, I like to work for chaplain."

The officer nodded and clapped Shang Ik on the shoulder with an approving grin. "All right. Follow me."

Chaplain's Boy

Shang Ik stumbled over his feet as he jogged behind the officer. The man moved at a brisk pace, whistling while he walked. Eventually the two entered a small chapel on the base and then a chaplain's office. Behind the desk sat a man who looked to Shang Ik to be in his midthirties, a soldier with blond hair and tall stature.

The officer gave two quick knocks on the doorjamb and stepped into the small office. "Chaplain Vajda, good afternoon. I hope you're getting settled in nicely."

The chaplain smiled and stood from his chair, coming around the front of the desk to salute and then shake the officer's hand. "Yes, Captain, I am adjusting to things here just fine. I've been unpacking some of my belongings and setting up my office."

The officer nodded and then turned and motioned toward Shang Ik, who had hung back outside the office door. "This young man is looking for work. I told him you had just arrived and might need some assistance. He says he'd like to work for you. What do you think?"

The chaplain extended his hand toward Shang Ik with a pleasant smile. "Hello. My name is Eduard Vajda."

Shang Ik timidly shook the chaplain's hand.

The officer cleared his throat. "I'm sorry. I forgot the young man's name. What was your name again, son?"

"Shang Ik Moon."

Chaplain Vajda nodded, still shaking Shang Ik's hand. "Ah, Moon. That should be easy enough to remember."

The captain and Chaplain Vajda shared a laugh while Shang Ik fidgeted nervously.

Chaplain Vajda let go of Shang Ik's hand and cleared his throat. "Tell me, Moon. Do you know who I am?"

The boy's heart raced as he shifted his gaze from the captain to the chaplain. The chaplain tapped his finger on a tiny silver cross he had pinned to the lapel of his uniform.

"Do you know what this is?" he asked gently.

The cross ignited his memory, and Shang Ik exhaled with relief. He remembered that Whan Soo had a necklace just like that pin. The cross was something Christians wore. He gave a wide smile and nodded his head.

"Oh! You Christian pastor!"

The chaplain broke out in a smile and nodded in the affirmative. "That's right. I am a pastor. Do you go to church?"

Shang Ik didn't know if he should tell the man the truth or if he should embellish for a better outcome. *Every time I have told the truth, it went well for me. No use to start lying now.*

"I go to church with my friend. He takes me there."

Chaplain Vajda nodded while the captain observed them quietly. "Well, that's wonderful. I know some of the earliest missionaries to Korea were Presbyterian. Was it a Presbyterian church?"

Shang Ik shook his head. "I not know, sir."

"Hmmm…Perhaps it was a Methodist church?"

Again he could only shake his head, not having any idea what those words meant anyway.

"Was it a Catholic church?"

At that word, Shang Ik perked up. *Catholic* was a well-known word, although Shang Ik wasn't entirely sure what it meant. The boy shook his head vigorously. "Me no Catholic!"

The captain and chaplain both laughed at the boy's firm response.

"Well, then that's good because I'm a Protestant chaplain, so I couldn't have a Catholic boy work for me. We'd have to send you to work for the Catholic chaplain." Chaplain Vajda put his hand on Shang Ik's shoulder and patted it gently. "That's fine, son. You'll work for me."

He thought he understood what the chaplain had said, and with his gentle touch, Shang Ik's breathing steadied, and his shoulders relaxed. As the chaplain and the captain continued speaking to each other, Shang Ik's gaze shifted to the floor. He allowed a long-forgotten sense of calm to wash over him. *This is good. I can work now. This is a good thing.*

From that day forward, Shang Ik assisted Chaplain Vajda in small tasks. He would run messages to and fro. He helped unpack the chaplain's boxes and set up his office. He cleaned and kept tidy the little chapel where the men would meet the chaplain for prayer and counseling. All the men in the Fifty- First Fighter Wing knew Chaplain Vajda, and his door was always open for the airmen and officers on the base.

Shang Ik offered little information about himself to the chaplain. He was always willing to do whatever task was asked of him.

He never wanted to seem ungrateful for the opportunity. In truth he was grateful, and his expressions of gratitude warmed the chaplain to him more and more with each passing day. As Shang Ik became attached to Chaplain Vajda, he started calling him Chapy as a term of endearment, and in turn, Chaplain Vajda called him Moon.

One day, Shang Ik came into the chaplain's office after delivering a message to the officer's quarters. When he entered the office, the chaplain was waiting for him with a serious expression.

"Moon, come here and have a seat. I want to talk to you."

Shang Ik immediately sat, but he began to perspire, anticipating the worst.

"Moon, why do you never go out and get your lunch at lunch hour? During lunch, I go to the mess hall, but I don't see where you go. Why don't you go to lunch?"

Shang Ik's cheeks reddened, but he had no choice but to answer honestly. "I have no money to buy lunch, Chapy."

Chaplain Vajda pursed his lips and observed the boy who had answered, while Shang Ik turned his gaze to the floor.

Shang Ik continued. "Chapy, office is long walk from front gate. The runway goes through middle of base. I go around. It takes me nearly an hour to go to Suwon to buy food and another hour to come back. It takes too long, so I stay here."

Chaplain Vajda shook his head. "I see. But what do you eat every day, Moon?"

Shang Ik swallowed hard and took a deep breath. "Chapy, there is big dump where air force throws the trash and garbage. I eat with the other children there, what the base throws away."

At that Chaplain Vajda lowered his head. Then he stood and walked over to his desk. Leaning over, he wrote something on a piece of paper, folded it, and handed it to Shang Ik. "Take this to the mess sergeant at the officer's dining hall."

Shang Ik stood and took the letter, relieved that the uncomfortable conversation had come to an end. "OK, Chapy, I go right now."

He took the letter and jogged over to the officers' dining hall. He tapped lightly on the mess hall door and handed the letter to the sergeant who answered. The sergeant took the letter and read it quickly.

Then he looked up at the boy in front of him. "Oh, you're the chaplain's boy?"

Shang Ik nodded, proud of the title. "Yes, sir. I am chaplain's boy."

The sergeant nodded, rubbing the stubble on his chin with his palm. He held the door open. "Well, come in. Come in, boy."

Shang Ik followed the sergeant, who led him to a table near the kitchen. Most of the soldiers were gone except for a few stragglers.

"Sit here." The sergeant gave his command and disappeared into the kitchen.

Shang Ik obediently sat and waited. *I wonder what the chaplain wanted in that letter.*

A few minutes later, the mess hall sergeant returned. In his arms he held a large tray piled high with food. At the sight of the food, the boy's eyes widened. It was more food than he had ever seen in one sitting.

He pointed to the tray. "I take this to Chaplain?"

The sergeant set down the tray and shook his head. "No, you eat this."

Shang Ik stared at the tray for a moment and then back up at the sergeant. The man smiled at him.

Shang Ik shook his head, certain he hadn't heard correctly. "Me eat?"

The sergeant's smile grew wider, and he laughed. He pushed the tray closer to the boy and handed him a fork. "Yes," he whispered, "you eat." He turned and left Shang Ik alone with his food.

Shang Ik only sat there, staring at the tray piled high with beef, apple pie, vegetables, and mashed potatoes. With trembling hands, he lifted the fork and began to consume his first real meal in nearly three years.

The first bite, through trembling lips, proved overwhelming, and he set down the fork and lowered his head. Tears sprung from his eyes, and he put his head in his hand, overcome with emotion.

He had no expectation that he would ever eat a real meal again. For the past three years, he had been surviving on whatever scraps came his way. He had no plans for his future beyond the survival of the moment. Swallowing, he composed himself and continued eating, savoring every bite.

That meal satisfied him throughout that day and into the following day. As lunchtime came the next day, Chaplain Vajda came in from his own lunch to see Shang Ik sitting in the office.

"Did you go eat today, Moon?"

Shang Ik shook his head, unsure of what he meant. "No. I'm supposed to eat again today, Chapy?"

Chaplain Vajda stopped in the middle of removing his jacket, his eyes wide. "Why of course! I made arrangements for you to eat at the mess hall every day. Didn't you take the sergeant my letter?"

Shang Ik nodded his head but wasn't sure if the chaplain understood what he was asking. "Are you sure he's going to give me more food, Chapy?"

Chaplain Vajda laughed and came to Shang Ik, gently pushing him out the door. "Don't you worry about that, Moon. Just go. Go enjoy your lunch."

Shang Ik obeyed and made his way to the officer's dining hall, but his own skepticism kept him from any feelings of excitement. *This must be a mistake. Surely the chaplain doesn't think I can just eat for free here every day. Not with all the food they give. Chaplain must be making a mistake. I won't embarrass him when they send me away.*

Shang Ik tapped tentatively on the mess hall door, thinking of the best way to make a request he was sure would be denied.

The mess hall sergeant came to the door and smiled warmly. "Hello, chaplain's boy! Come on in." He gestured for Shang Ik to enter and then pointed to an empty table before returning to the kitchen.

A few minutes later, the sergeant returned with a tray. On the tray, there seemed to be even more food than the day before. The sergeant set the tray carefully before the boy. Then he handed him his utensils and left him alone.

Shang Ik stared as steam floated overtop the hot meal. Something strange occurred to him as he tried to force himself to mentally accept that this was his new normal. It occurred to him that, in all this time, he had been waiting to die.

The unnerving expectation that death would be coming for him had been his constant companion since the moment he learned of his father's death. Everything he had experienced since then—his mother's fate, his sister's tragedy, his niece slowly fading away in front of him, along with the constant fear of attack by some military force—had surrounded him with the expectation that death lurked just outside his doorstep. He had proof of this: starvation was the experience of dying a little every day.

For the past few years, Shang Ik had experienced incremental death. The meal before him was hinting to him that a shift of sorts was occurring, and he had to slow down to process it. The same military that had killed his sister was now feeding him delicious meals every day. He had to let the food sit for a while as he digested it, along with this new reality. It began to dawn on him that so much of what he thought was his future was now his past.

Wondering where his next meal was coming from, how he would survive, or if he would make it from one week to the next, all that was over. As the weight of starvation lifted off his chest and his world flooded with the possibilities of what could be, he stopped eating. His hands fell into his lap.

He was exhausted. He didn't know for sure what weight he had been carrying, but he suddenly felt it lift, and he was weak. The tray of food sat before him, welcoming and savory. It was so plentiful that he felt his soul break. *Who was looking out for me? Why was I given so much when others just outside this gate were struggling for survival as I had been? Why me?*

He lifted the fork and began to eat with a gratitude that touched his soul. He allowed the food to rejuvenate him. He left the mess hall after his meal, and every step felt lighter. The sky seemed bluer and the trees greener. He felt the vibrant pulse of life around him for the first time in what seemed like forever. He could fully appreciate being alive because he wasn't primarily concerned with staying alive.

For the next few days, he asked the chaplain if he were sure he could eat again the next day. The chaplain would nod his head with joking exasperation.

"Yes, Moon, every day at noon you go and eat your lunch. Keep eating that way and you'll get nice and fat."

Shang Ik and Chaplain Vajda soon developed a beautiful friendship. The chaplain's curiosity about the boy increased, and Shang Ik's trust in the chaplain led him to share everything about himself. He told the chaplain about his parents and how he had lived with his grandmother in North Korea before coming to Seoul.

He told him what his father did, about the war, and how he lost his stepmother and *Eomma-Azumm*a. He shared what happened to his sister and how he had almost died several times before he turned sixteen. He was relieved to have someone to share about the airplane attacks and how he had gotten caught in the front line between the South Koreans and Chinese.

Every day they would talk about the things Shang Ik had experienced. Saying these painful memories out loud would sometimes overwhelm Shang Ik. He hadn't stopped to consider all the tragedies he had experienced in such a short time. He was only sixteen, but he felt sixty.

One day, Chaplain Vajda and Shang Ik were walking through the base. Shang Ik could see that something was troubling the chaplain, but he didn't want to pry.

After walking a few moments in silence, the chaplain finally blurted out. "Moon, I've never asked this question, but where do you sleep?"

Shang Ik looked at the chaplain curiously. "I sleep outside the military base. There is little refugee tent there."

They walked together a few more moments. A brisk winter wind chilled their faces.

"Aren't you cold?" the chaplain asked after a minute.

Shang Ik hesitated but answered truthfully. "Yes, it is cold. And there is no stove, just the tent. We don't have beds, so we lay on the floor close together to stay warm."

They continued their walk in silence, Shang Ik feeling no more shame with the chaplain. He simply waited patiently to see what the military man would say next.

"I'd like to see the tent, if you don't mind showing it to me."

Shang Ik nodded, motioning toward the gate. "I can show you right now, Chapy."

Together they left the base and walked toward the refugee tent. As they passed the dump, some children holding their buckets of discarded food waved their hands and greeted Shang Ik. He gave a warm smile and waved back. He felt guilty. He had been given so much, and they had so little. Chaplain Vajda remained solemn, simply observing as he walked.

They reached the tent and Shang Ik led the chaplain toward the area where he slept, just a bare floor with no stove and no way to keep warm.

"Aren't you cold in here through the night?" the chaplain asked.

"Oh, I curl up like a ball all night to keep my body heat," replied Shang Ik.

The few people who were there during the day stared at the tall, blond-haired man. Chaplain Vajda simply nodded when Shang Ik showed him where he lay his head every night.

They were silent the entire way back to the base. Once they reached the chaplain's office, he turned to Shang Ik. "You know, maybe we should have you come and live at the base chapel. There is a little room, a sacristy, in the back. You can sleep there. How would that sound?"

Shang Ik couldn't believe what he heard. He tried not to appear too eager, fearing the chaplain might change his mind. *That would be too good to be true.*

"I would like that, Chapy."

"Come with me. We'll see about it."

The chaplain turned quickly and trotted off toward the office of the supply officer on the base. After some light conversation, he was able to acquire a military cot, a mattress, blankets, and sheets. Together Chaplain Vajda and Shang Ik carried the supplies to the little room behind the chapel.

The room had some boxes and religious memorabilia, but together they quickly worked to clear the space. Shang Ik was dressing the bed with the sheets, amazed at how quickly this blessing had come upon him, when the chaplain came in with a box in his hand.

"Here, Moon, I found this radio. I thought you might like to listen to some music in the evenings so it won't be so lonesome out here."

Shang Ik stared in awe at the little black device. Radio was a luxury. He couldn't believe he had one of his own. He reached out and slowly took it. A lump formed in his throat.

Sensing that he was becoming overwhelmed, Chaplain Vajda turned to leave Shang Ik. As he left the little room, he turned around to deliver one last bit of news. "Oh, by the way, since you'll be living on the base now, you'll need all three meals here. So make sure you report to the mess hall first thing in the morning for your breakfast." With that, he gently closed the door and left Shang Ik sitting in disbelief.

Clutching the little black radio, he sat on the edge of his cot, the military issue bedsheets and blanket crisp and clean beneath him. It was warm, cozy, and quiet. The chapel on the other side of his door gave him a feeling of safety. He turned the switch on the radio and let the music fill the empty room.

Laying his head on the pillow, he exhaled slowly and tried to absorb the gifts he had been given. *I didn't earn any of this. I didn't pay for this cot or this warm room. And it's all mine. I don't buy my food. And I'll be eating even more!*

He remembered the blood, sweat, labor, and tears he had squandered in Mr. Kim's farmhouse, how he had been repaid with mistreatment and hatred. All his efforts there had given him nothing. And none of his efforts here had given him so much. What was this phenomenon?

He recalled a conversation he and Chapy had shared after Shang Ik's third or fourth meal at the mess hall.

"Chapy, how can I have this food when I haven't paid for it? They give me so much every day. How can this be right?"

Chaplain Vajda smiled and chuckled, as if he were warming up to his favorite subject. "Ahh, Shang Ik, that is what we call grace. Grace is when we receive something that we don't deserve."

Shang Ik felt confused. He hadn't been taught to expect something for nothing. "But why do you give grace to me?"

Chaplain Vajda leaned forward, clasping his hands together. "Because God gave grace to me. He gave it to me, so I can give it to you. And maybe one day, you can give it to someone else."

Shang Ik lay on his cot now in the little sacristy, contemplating Chapy's words. He had lived so long falling a little deeper into hell every day. But in a matter of a few days, so much of that hell seemed behind him. *If grace is what Chapy has done, then grace is a good thing indeed. Maybe it's something I can try.*

He closed his eyes, still clutching the little black radio as Eddie Fisher singing "I'm Walking Behind You" lulled him to sleep.

Seoul Searching

Shang Ik hummed as he strolled through the tiny chapel in the Fifty-First Fighter Interceptor Wing of the American air force base near Suwon. Holding a stack of small Bibles and some hymnal pamphlets, he moved along each row, setting a Bible and a pamphlet on each seat. Chaplain Vajda liked everything to be set up right after breakfast so anyone who came to the chapel early would find what he needed.

He thumbed through the pages of the Bible as he walked, trying to look for words he recognized and sounding out words he didn't. He turned to the book of Ephesians, to a passage he had found highlighted in other pieces of literature he had seen in the chaplain's office, Ephesians 2:4.

"But God, w-w-wh who is r-r-rich in…mercy, b-b-be-cause of His g-gr-great love with which He loved us."

A slam interrupted his stammering, and he quickly set down the Bible and continued his task.

Chaplain Vajda poked his head in and smiled when he saw Shang Ik. "Ah, there you are, Moon! I wanted to talk to you."

Shang Ik set down the Bibles and pamphlets as the chaplain approached him.

"Suwon is having some kind of town meeting tonight. I've received permission to attend the meeting and speak to the gathering there. I'd like you to come and be my interpreter."

Shang Ik thought for a moment. "Interpreter, Chapy? What's interpreter?"

Chaplain Vajda rubbed his chin as he thought. "Well, let's see. An interpreter means you would tell them in Korean what I am saying in English. You would translate my words into Korean so they can understand me."

Shang Ik's eyes widened, and he held up his hands, shaking his head. "No, no, Chapy! My English not so good yet! I'm not sure I can do that."

Chaplain Vajda smiled and placed his hands on Shang Ik's shoulder. "Come, Moon. It's better than nothing. It's better that they understand a little bit from you than not understand anything at all. Don't you agree?"

Shang Ik sighed. *Chapy might be very disappointed if the people don't understand his message. Maybe I should do it. He's done a lot for me.*

"All right, Chapy. I go with you. I be interpreter."

Chaplain Vajda's smile widened as he slapped Shang Ik's shoulder. "Good! I'll make the arrangements, and we'll leave later this afternoon."

He turned and practically skipped out of the chapel. Shang Ik watched him for a moment. Then he picked up the Bible and flipped back to Ephesians 2:4. "But God, w-w-wh who is r-r-rich in mercy…"

Later that afternoon he sat, holding one hand over his eyes to protect them from the dust that was flying into the jeep. The chaplain sat next to him, one hand hanging out the window and the other hand holding his Bible in his lap. Two armed guards rode in the front for their protection. Chaplain Vajda could not suppress a grin as he peered out the window of the jeep, waving his hand periodically to passersby.

He is so happy to be doing this. What if I make a mistake? What if I say the wrong thing? What if no one cares about Chapy's message because I don't know what he's saying? Fidgeting in his seat, Shang Ik tugged at his collar and tapped his foot.

The chaplain noticed the fidgeting and laughed, clapping Shang Ik on his shoulder. "Don't be nervous, Moon! We'll be in and out quickly. We're just going to share the message of the gospel, not preach a long sermon. You'll do fine."

Shang Ik nodded and forced a smile. "OK, Chapy!"

This makes him so happy. It's like all he wants to do in life is talk to people about his God. It's so strange.

The jeep pulled into the town of Suwon and came to a stop before the city hall building. As he stepped out of the jeep, Shang Ik paused. The white tarp was gone, but the corner against the building where he had spent his first night in Suwon was still there.

His hand involuntarily came up to his chest, and he realized his heart was racing. He wasn't sure if it was because of his nerves or the memory of that first night sleeping under a tent, unsure where his next meal was coming from.

Chaplain Vajda's voice snapped him back to attention. "Come on, Moon. We'll be speaking in the city square."

Shang Ik followed the chaplain toward a small podium that had been set up. He hadn't noticed when he first exited the jeep, but now his eyes took in the size of the crowd, and his heart would not stop racing. At least 150 people were present—some sitting and others standing. All were attentive, waiting to hear what the tall, white-skinned man was going to say.

Shang Ik followed Chapy through the crowd with trembling hands and weak knees, his eyes to the ground. The chaplain stepped onto the small wooden platform, and Shang Ik followed. The wooden planks creaked under their weight, but at this moment, falling was the least of Shang Ik's concerns.

Chaplain Vajda smiled broadly and, holding his Bible in his hand, began to speak. "Hello! I've come here today to speak to you all about hope. I know we've all been around this war for a long time. We've seen many terrible things. We've all had moments of despair and sadness. But there is something that can comfort us even in those moments!" Chaplain Vajda took a breath and looked at Shang Ik.

Shang Ik swallowed and then turned to address the crowd in his native Korean. "This man says we can have hope. That many bad things happen. The war is bad. But we can be comforted."

Chaplain Vajda nodded his approval and continued. "We know all too much the evil imagination of people who bring war. Many of us suffer because of their plans. Most of us have no say in the decision to go to war. But I know this: you are not my enemy. And I am not your enemy. I have a God who says we are all his children! There is hope in the Son of God. God sent His Son to earth to save us from our sins and to bring us healing from the sins of others. With God there is hope!"

Shang Ik stared wide-eyed at the chaplain, struggling to understand. When he was finished, he quickly gave his best summation of the message to the crowd. "Many have suffered in this war. We are not one another's enemies. Maybe we all suffer in war. But this man says he has a God, and we are the children of that God. And that God is rich! He has much mercy, and he is rich in mercy and love! That is the hope this man speaks."

Many people in the crowd cocked their heads and leaned forward, seemingly interested in what was being said. Bolstered by their response, Chaplain Vajda continued speaking more vigorously, and Shang Ik interpreted the message as best as he could.

When the twenty-minute appeal was over, Shang Ik and the chaplain hopped off the makeshift podium as people wandered away. Shang Ik took out his handkerchief and mopped the sweat off his brow. As he did, a very distinguished-looking middle-aged man made his way to the chaplain and Shang Ik.

"Hello, Chaplain, I am a professor of English at Yeon-Se University. It is one of the largest universities in Korea." The man leaned in as he shook the chaplain's hand. "Ivy League university," the man said, emphasizing the importance of the university and himself.

Chaplain Vajda nodded and smiled, motioning toward Shang Ik. "What did you think of my interpreter?"

Shang Ik immediately began to tremble as he stood next to the chaplain. *He teaches English! He'll tell the chaplain I didn't know what I was saying!*

But the man laughed and tapped the boy's shoulder. "Well, kid, you did pretty good."

Shang Ik's shoulders collapsed as he sighed with relief. In the jeep on their way back to the base, Shang Ik turned to Vajda. "Chapy, you think you can teach English to me?"

The chaplain looked at Shang Ik with a pleased smile. Then he lifted his chin and took a deep breath. "Well, there aren't any textbooks on base, Moon. There are no schoolbooks."

Shang Ik nodded and looked down at his hands. He felt Chapy place his hand on his shoulder, and he looked up to see him leaning in toward Shang Ik's face.

"But maybe you can learn from something else."

The following day Shang Ik came into the chaplain's office first thing in the morning, per the chaplain's instructions. When he entered the room, Chaplain Vajda was sitting on a chair with his hands folded beneath his chin, his eyes closed.

Shang Ik stared at him for a few moments and then quietly rapped on the doorway. "I'm here, Chapy."

The older man's eyes popped open, and without looking at Shang Ik, he stood up. He pointed to the chair and then moved over to his bookcase. Shang Ik sat in the chair as Vajda removed a small book from the shelf and then came and sat next to Shang Ik.

"Moon, do you know what this is?"

Shang Ik took the little book in his hands and turned it over. The cover read *Luther's Small Catechism.* Shang Ik shook his head. "I not know, Chapy."

The man nodded. "This is a book about what Christians believe, specifically Lutherans like myself. We believe in God, the creator of the universe and all living things, including you and me. Do you understand?"

It took Shang Ik a moment to respond. *I know he is talking about his God. I only remember some things from what I heard about Christians. I don't understand everything about their God, but if I ask him, I might offend him.*

"Yes, Chapy, I think I understand."

The chaplain continued, settling into the role of a teacher. "You see, Moon, I've been wanting to take the time to talk to you about what I believe, about God and life. But we've been so busy that there just never seemed to be an opportunity. But you asked me to help you with your English so I think this is a good way to begin."

Shang Ik nodded. "I see, Chapy. You teach me English with God books."

The chaplain nodded his head and smiled. "That's right, Moon! I can use the books I have here and explain to you more about

God, and in the meantime, you'll be working on your English. Because these are the only books I have on the base, it's really the best I can do. Is that all right with you?"

Shang Ik nodded but remained silent. *I'm not so sure if I want to learn about this God. What is the point?* He fidgeted nervously, unsure how to respond. His mind returned to a memory of a few years ago, sitting on a snowy mountain in the dead of night. *That night I thought about God, about a superhero with me. It made me feel less alone, whether it was real or not. It helped me rest.*

He looked up at the chaplain, who was waiting patiently to see what he would say. *Maybe I can learn about the chaplain's God. Who knows what it is all about? Maybe it's harmless, or perhaps it really means something. Either way, one thing I know is that the chaplain is a good man. If his beliefs help him be who he is, maybe I can learn about them too.*

Chaplain Vajda leaned over to Shang Ik and spoke softly, not wanting to pressure him. "Well, Moon, what do you think? Would you like to learn English this way? Would you like me to teach you about God?"

Shang Ik nodded and opened the small book. "Yes, Chapy, I want you to teach me. I want to learn. Teach me from the little book."

Eduard Vajda smiled, took the book from the boy's hand, and opened it to the Lord's Prayer. He began to slowly read out loud. "Our Father, who art in Heaven, hallowed be your name…"

Shang Ik and Chaplain Vajda met every day from that point on to read from *Luther's Small Catechism* or the Bible. As Shang Ik's English improved, so did his knowledge of the chaplain's God. Shang Ik would accompany Chaplain Vajda on his trips to neighboring towns. Together they visited orphanages and hospitals, sharing the gospel. As he did, Shang Ik's heart began to turn more and more toward his Chapy's God.

He learned of a belief that said it was his duty to care for the poor, the orphaned, the sick, and the widowed. It was the exact opposite of how he had been treated. He learned of a belief that said people were more important than politics and foreign policy. He saw a man from another land treat his people with more kindness and dignity than he had ever seen anyone treated. The more he saw, the more his heart turned toward a God who inspired people to care for others more than themselves.

"Moon, God made mankind in His image. Every human being carried a part of God. God values all His creation, even the birds of the sky and the trees and the animals. But He especially values us. We are of deep importance to God, His greatest treasure."

Shang Ik listened with open-minded curiosity, although this concept was new. *If God is so powerful, then why would he value silly things like birds and trees? Or me?*

"He so values us that He wanted to resolve the issue of sin, this issue of the things we do to ourselves and one another that keep us separate from Him. Things like war and slavery and abuse. Things like violence. Like what you and I have seen here."

Shang Ik shook his head at that. He certainly had seen enough of what human beings could do.

"God values us, but He also values the free will that He gave us. And He allows us to become part of His plan to restore everything back to its original purpose. A purpose where we function as creation of God, where we treat every living creature as having the value that God has placed on it."

The more Chapy spoke with passion about the concept of God, the more Shang Ik began to realize that the idea that he had value to God affected his own perception of himself. He felt strange thinking less of himself and even stranger thinking less of other people.

One day as they returned in the jeep from visiting a local orphanage, Chaplain Vajda turned to Shang Ik with an oddly comical expression on his face. "Moon, I want you to consider becoming a preacher."

Shang Ik smirked and shook his head, trying not to sound too incredulous. "Ha! You are funny, Chapy."

"No, I'm serious, Moon. I see the way you interpret. I've picked up some Korean phrases, and I know you are explaining God to people in a way they will understand. You aren't just going through the motions. You care. That is the heart of a preacher."

"A preacher, Chapy? Why a preacher? I always thought of becoming a scientist. My father wanted me to be a lawyer like him, but I wanted to be a scientist, like the ones who made the atomic bomb." He smiled as he explained this to the chaplain, spreading his hands to show an explosion. He was still fascinated with Hiroshima.

Chaplain Vajda ignored his gesture and leaned in further. "Moon, you and I have seen many tragic things in this war. You more than me. You have seen how God's creation can do terrible things. You have also seen how we can hurt and destroy one another. I truly believe that this breaks God's heart."

Shang Ik stopped making faces when he noticed Chapy had grown emotional. He was clearly overcome.

"I've explained to you about how God gave humans free will. That means we are truly free to live our lives and to make choices that affect other people, and sometimes He chooses not to stop those choices even though they lead to pain and suffering. That is because He honors our freedom as creation to build the life we want, whether good or bad."

He took a deep breath and continued. "But there are some moments where He does step in. Does He step in because He loves some more than others? No! He is not a respecter of persons. He doesn't love any of us more than anyone else. But there are clearly times when He does step in. Why is that? Why does He spare some and not others?"

Shang Ik looked down at his hand as a lump formed in his throat. *Doesn't he know that I've been struggling with this question for years? Doesn't he know that I already feel guilty? Why is he making me feel more shame than I already feel?*

"Moon, I've told you that you are special to God. And that's true. You are incredibly special to God. But so is everyone. You aren't more special than anyone else is. And yet your life was spared. Not once or twice but several times. God loves every one of his creation. And yet some people die while others live. Don't you think it's a good idea to figure out the reason you were spared?"

Shang Ik kept his eyes down as he pondered the heavy line of questioning. *If what Chapy says is true, why would God have a purpose for me and not for everyone else? It doesn't make any sense.*

Almost as if he read his mind, Chapy placed his hand on Shang Ik's shoulder and squeezed hard.

"God has a purpose for all His children, Moon. But He is also sovereign. That means He knows things that we don't, and sometimes His ways are something we will never understand this side of heaven. But just because He doesn't always intervene and make every choice right and ease every bit of suffering, this doesn't mean He isn't yearning for His children, yearning to bring restoration to this world, and making plans that will lead to His healing being established on the earth for all men. How do you know that you aren't a part of those plans?"

Shang Ik felt overwhelmed, weighed down by the pain of guilt he had been carrying all his life, guilt that he was a burden, guilt that he didn't deserve to live when so many others had perished around him. He wanted to make it better for himself, but the pain in his heart didn't allow him to see the way clearly.

"Chapy, you think I can be part of God's plan to make this all better? To make this right?"

The chaplain smiled and nodded his head. "Moon, I absolutely guarantee it."

They continued the ride back to the base in silence, but Shang Ik could not shake the conversation they had. The idea of redeeming the loss was such a draw for Shang Ik. *What a wonderful gift that would be, to be able to bring restoration to someone...anyone! To do good. To be of value to someone the way Chapy was of value to me.*

Day after day, the chaplain attempted to persuade Shang Ik to become a preacher. As Shang Ik progressed in his English and his understanding of the doctrine of Christianity, Chaplain Vajda grew in his enthusiasm about Shang Ik's future.

"I can send you to Concordia Seminary in Saint Louis, Missouri, in the United States, where I went to study to become a Lutheran pastor. Of course, you have to first go to a college to prepare for the entrance to the seminary. You can study and become a pastor, and one day you can return to Korea and be a missionary to your own people. What do you think of that?"

Shang Ik shook his head as he and Chapy piled their trays with food in the mess hall. "But, Chapy, I don't think I can go to America. My English not so good, and Korea is my home."

"It would only be temporary, Moon. You would return here as soon as your studies are over. You've made such good progress. I know you would do well in seminary. You'd make a wonderful pastor."

Shang Ik shrugged as he carried his tray to their table. The chaplain said no more, and Shang Ik could tell he was beginning to wonder if his words were falling on deaf ears.

But Shang Ik was not deaf. Every night he would go over Chaplain Vajda's words as he lay in the cot in his little room behind the chapel. At only seventeen, he felt he had lived a lifetime. As much as he had suffered, when he thought of the people who surrounded him who were still suffering, his people, he could not help but feel blessed beyond measure. He felt almost too blessed.

Although he was quickly stepping into adulthood, he was not so eager to live his own life. He was more eager to pay some of the grace he had received forward. He wanted to do good, but he didn't know where to begin.

One night not long after that, he lay in his cot, contemplating the complete turnaround that was occurring in his life in just a few short months. Keeping his unhealthy habit of not processing his feelings, Shang Ik had intentionally not brought to mind much of his past pain.

But tonight he purposefully began to go over the past few months. He remembered feeling so lost, so desperate, and so hopeless. And now in a complete turnaround, he felt full of possibility. He was cared for and provided for. He had hope and a future. Nothing would ever erase the feeling of having lost everyone he loved. But he did feel for the first time in what felt like a lifetime that happiness was a possibility. His soul felt restored.

Much of that had to do with Chapy, his kindness and the expressions of his love. He went so much out of his way to restore the life of a boy he didn't know and to make restitution and bring hope to many orphans, widows, and people in need. There wasn't a person in Shang Ik's life who had ever taught him this value until he met Chapy. And now he wanted to become the person who brought light into darkness because Chapy's light saved him from his own darkness.

I don't understand much about God or who God is. Maybe I'm not even fully certain if it's real. But I know what is real. Chapy is real, and what he's done for me and the other orphans here is real. And if I can learn to do what he did, then I can make my life better. If that comes from God, so be it. Whatever causes that light, I need to be a part of it. And I need to bring it to my people.

The next morning, he raced through the base at breakneck speed, kicking his long legs and smiling. He hadn't run so carefree since he was scaring chickens in his grandmother's village. He burst through Chaplain Vajda's office, causing the man to jump in his seat and drop the papers he was holding to the ground.

"Moon! What are you doing? What's wrong?"

"Chapy! I want you to send me to school. I want to be pastor and a preacher like you. I want to study so I can learn about God's light and come back here to share it with my people."

Chapy paused from gathering his scattered paperwork, breaking into a smile as he jumped up and rushed to him. Placing both hands on Shang Ik's shoulders, he looked him in the eye, trying to be firm but clearly struggling to hide his joy. "Are you sure, Moon? It means a lot of hard work, you know. You would have to study very hard. You might be homesick."

Shang Ik nodded enthusiastically. "I want to do it. Please write to those colleges you told me about. I want to learn to be a pastor so I can help my people the way you helped me. I want to do it, Chapy."

Chaplain Vajda laughed and pulled Shang Ik into his arms for a bear hug. "All right, Moon. I'll write to the colleges and let you know when we have a response. In the meantime, we'll continue studying and getting you ready for college and seminary."

Shang Ik nodded and smiled, his eagerness spilling over onto everything he touched. He was more excited about going to America than the chaplain had ever seen him about anything.

For months they worked, increasing Shang Ik's studies and waiting for a response from one of the schools to which the chaplain had written.

Shang Ik was beginning to lose hope that any college would respond. He grew more and more apprehensive until one afternoon they received a letter from Saint John's College in Winfield, Kansas.

Dear Chaplain Vajda,

We are pleased to inform you that we have decided to take on your young protégé as a student on scholarship at Saint John's College. We are pleased to partner with you to educate this young man in his chosen path and to equip him to serve one day in the Lutheran tradition.

Once his visa and immigration documents have been approved, we will move forward with enrollment.

When he read the letter containing the long-awaited good news, Shang Ik expected to feel excitement. But as Chapy took the letter, rereading its contents with glee, Shang Ik began to feel a sinking feeling in the pit of his stomach. Leaving Chapy with the letter, Shang Ik stood and slowly left the room.

Walking to the perimeter of the base, Shang Ik stared off into the distance at nearby towns and villages. He would be leaving Korea. *Will I ever see it again? Will I ever run its roads or see its snowy winters?* He took his time, wandering down the road near the base. Cherry blossoms swayed in the breeze, and he reached over to feel the white petals in his hands.

He passed by the refugee tent he used to live in, watching as children wandered in and out of the tent. They were aimless and idle instead of carefree and innocent. He had been one of them. Only their future was bleak, and he had been given this wonderful opportunity. And with the opportunity, there was a noble purpose. When he returned to the base, he went straight to the chaplain's office, not bothering to knock.

"Ah, Moon! There you are. I've been looking over the information from Saint John's, and I believe we can arrange for a meal plan for you—"

"Chapy," Shang Ik interrupted. "I would like you to take me to Seoul."

Chaplain Vajda stopped talking and looked up at Shang Ik. He set the letter on the desk and ran his hand through his blond hair. "Er, Moon, they've imposed martial law on the city of Seoul. That means only military personnel can go in and out. The city...it's not what it used to be."

Shang Ik stepped forward, placing both hands on the chaplain's desk. "I understand, Chapy. But please, I need to go to Seoul. Before I leave for America, I have to know if there's anything else I can know about my family. It's time I know for sure, and it has to happen before I leave."

Chaplain Vajda blinked a few times, surprised. Then he slowly nodded as Shang Ik turned and walked out of the room, closing the door behind him.

Resurrection City

Something in the air in Seoul gave Shang Ik a sick feeling. The stench of sulfur still wafted in the breeze from the rubble that had been many of Seoul's prominent buildings. The bombing and gunfire that had flattened the city left its mark tattooed on anything left standing. Storefronts and homes were defaced with bullet holes, and whole sides were missing from many buildings. Bombings and army tanks had torn apart entire blocks where apartments once stood. The face of the once lively and hopeful city was completely distorted. Shang Ik leaned his head out the jeep window as they approached the military checkpoint. His heart broke for his city. The US Army had primary control of the area of Seoul at this point.

Chaplain Vajda leaned out the window as they approached the checkpoint. "Officer

Eduard Vajda, Chaplain Corps. This young man is my interpreter."

The officer checked Chaplain Vajda's identification and then peered suspiciously at Shang Ik. After looking them both up and down, he nodded sternly and waved them through. The drive into Seoul was quiet and solemn. The chaplain didn't pepper Shang Ik with questions, mostly leaving him to his thoughts as Shang Ik stared out the window, struggling to conceal his emotions.

Most of the buildings were now rubble, and there were no distinguishable landmarks. Smoke still rose in the city from various points of intense artillery fire. As they drove through what had been Seoul, the weight of the entire war seemed concentrated in this one area.

Once the potholes in the roads became too difficult to navigate, they exited the jeep and continued on foot. Shang Ik peered around, one hand above his eyes, trying to get his bearings. The street signs were gone, and trying to find his old house seemed impossible without familiar buildings. He and the chaplain approached different people as they walked, trying to get directions to the area where Shang Ik had lived with his parents.

After a few dead ends, one man was kind enough to point them toward the general area of Shang Ik's former residence. Shang Ik picked up the pace, scared but eager to see what had become of the place of his fondest memories. Breaking into a jog, Shang Ik rounded the corner where his favorite open market once stood and came to a sudden halt before what was once his home. His knees trembled as his hands fell to his sides.

The entire house had been leveled. Only a flat plane of rubble and debris lay where his home once stood. Gripping his chest with his hand, he walked up to the pile of wood, cement, and other materials, scanning to see if anything familiar jumped out at him—an old family photo, a favorite book, a record, an old toy— anything to connect him with that past life. Lifting pieces of cement and chunks of wood, he could find nothing recognizable.

Chaplain Vajda stayed down by the street as Shang Ik rummaged. Tears threatened to break through the young man's eyes and drip onto the flattened building. He composed himself after a few minutes and returned to the street.

"Let's go, Chapy. There's nothing here."

He and the chaplain continued walking in silence while Shang Ik looked around, trying to take everything in one last time before they had to leave.

Maneuvering the torn streets, they made it down the road a few paces when they came upon a woman standing before a home riddled with bullet holes. She had an old cart and was rummaging through the rubble, trying to salvage any bricks and building material that could be of use. Curious, Shang Ik approached her slowly. She raised her head as she prepared to toss a brick onto her pile, and their eyes met.

Shang Ik's eyebrows lifted with surprise. "Mrs. Chen?"

His old neighbor stared at him. Then she tossed the brick onto the pile and shook her head in disbelief. "You're alive?"

Shang Ik nodded but thought to himself, *Just barely*.

"Yes, I am alive."

She kept staring at him, shaking her head incredulously. Not knowing what else to say, Shang Ik shrugged his shoulders and turned to join Chaplain Vajda.

"Your mother thinks you are dead, you know."

Shang Ik's heart dropped as he froze in his tracks. He slowly turned to face Mrs. Chen. His breathing came out in shallow puffs. The chaplain stared at Shang Ik, looking confused.

Shang Ik slowly walked up to the woman, who had returned to rummaging through the pile of debris as if nothing had happened. *Did I hear her correctly?*

"Mrs. Chen, what did you just say?"

"Your mother. Oh, what did you call her? *Eomma-Azumma.* I spoke with her just the other day. She thinks you're dead."

Shang Ik inched toward the woman slowly, as if not wanting to scare her off. His instinct was to pounce on her and demand answers.

Holding his hands up, he controlled his breathing and spoke as calmly as possible. "Mrs. Chen, is *Eomma-Azumma* still alive?"

She nonchalantly tossed a two-by-four onto the pile and brushed off her hands. "Yes."

Chaplain Vajda watched as Shang Ik reached up to the woman on the pile of debris, gesturing wildly with his hands and speaking in Korean. He held up his hand as Shang Ik came running his way.

"Moon, what is happening? What's wrong?"

Shang Ik ran to the chaplain and placed both hands on his shoulders with tears streaming down his cheeks. "Chapy, my *eomma-azumma* is alive."

Shang Ik ran to the jeep with the chaplain close on his heels. Jumping into the car, the chaplain shifted into drive and started away from the building where they had parked.

"Chapy, she says *Eomma-Azumma* is staying with her friend here in Seoul! That is close to us. Turn left at this building. She said she smuggled herself in a week ago. Imagine, Chapy! Just one week ago! What a coincidence! Turn right after this road."

The chaplain jerked the wheel from left to right, struggling to keep up with Shang Ik's directions as his own excitement grew. "Moon, is this the woman who you said was like a mother to you? She used to make your suits?"

"She was more than that, Chapy! She would talk to me, listen to me, and give me advice. She was the only other person I could talk to besides *Appa*. And after he died and *Uibus-Eomi* couldn't keep me anymore, she was there for me! And when I thought the North Koreans had taken her, I was as sad as when *Appa* died."

"Moon, are you sure you know where she's staying? Or if it's even her? How do you know for sure that this lady you spoke to wasn't mistaken?"

Shang Ik smiled and laughed as he jumped up and down in his seat. "Chapy, that woman was our neighbor. She knew *Appa* and *Uibus-Eomi*, and she knew me. We would see each other often. She knew who *Eomma-Azumma* was. If she says she is alive and here in Seoul, then my *eomma-azumma* is here! Stop!"

The chaplain slammed on the brakes as Shang Ik pointed out the driver's side window. They were in a neighborhood that had missed most of the destruction. Some street signs and houses stood defiantly against the destruction so close by.

"This is the house where *Eomma-Azumma*'s friend lived. This must be where she's staying."

The chaplain looked at the modest home, incredulous that Shang Ik's loved one was alive and just as surprised the house had escaped the fate of buildings not far away. It had a small common yard in the center with houses all around. The assault from the North had not touched any of them. A small gate blocked their view of the courtyard.

Chaplain Vajda pursed his lips and rubbed his chin. Shaking his head, he mumbled to himself, "Imagine. If we wouldn't have gotten permission to come this week, you would have missed her."

But Shang Ik wasn't listening to the chaplain. He was staring at the little house and breathing heavily.

The chaplain turned to him and placed one hand on his shoulder. "Moon, you go ahead. Take your time, as much time as you need. I'll be here."

Shang Ik inhaled. Then he opened the passenger door and walked slowly around the jeep. He approached the gate of the home and opened it gingerly as he walked into the courtyard.

Upon walking through the gate, he came upon a woman standing in the middle of the courtyard, washing her face at the outdoor pump. She cupped her hands under the water she had pumped into a basin and splashed it on her face, rubbing gently.

As she was submerging her hands into the water one more time, she looked up. Her face lost all color as she stared at the tall young man at the entrance of the courtyard. He stared at her. The recognition and soul connection they shared washed over them like a tidal wave.

Shang Ik's hand gripped his chest as he managed to whisper, "*Eomma?*"

The woman said not a word, but lifting her trembling hands to her face, she doubled over and began to convulse.

Shang Ik ran to her and held her in his arms. "Oh, *Eomma*! My *eomma-azumma*, what did they do? What have they done to you?"

A sharp cry from her mouth interrupted his tearful questioning as her wailing and tears spilled out of her and mixed with the basin water. She touched his face, his chest, and his hair as she trembled and cried, her breath coming in short gasps. "My son! My son! My son!"

Shang Ik wept openly as he shook his head, caressing her face and wiping her tears. "Oh, *Eomma-Azumma,* I so often wished you were my *eomma* and I was your son, your real son."

She pushed him away from her and held him at arm's length. He tried to bring her in for a hug, but she kept him away as she shook her head, struggling to breathe through her tears.

"No, Shang Ik. No more. No more of this pain for me and these lies for you."

Shang Ik's heart broke with pity for her. *She's rambling. They must have tortured her horribly.* His tears fell as he rubbed her back.

"Shhhh, *Eomma-Azumma*. It's all right. Don't get excited. You're safe now. Everything will be all right."

She pushed herself away from him and stood to her feet. "No!"

Shang Ik jumped up and tried to keep her calm. "All right, *Eomma-Azumma*. All right. What is it you are trying to say? What do you mean no more lies?"

She clutched at her chest as she wept, spitting the words out through lips that had carried this secret for far too long. "I am your mother."

Shang Ik nodded. "Yes, *Eomma*. You are like a mother to me. You're the closest thing to a mother I have ever had."

She came close to him and touched his face. "No, Shang Ik. I am your mother. Chun-Soo and I agreed we would wait to tell you the truth until you got to know me better. But then he died, and the timing just wasn't right. Then the war came, and I never got the chance. But I'm telling you now. I am your mother. I am your mother, and you are my son."

At the mention of his father's name, Shang Ik stepped back. He snatched his hands away from hers as she reached for him.

"Shang Ik, when I met your father and we married, we were children. Not much older than you are now. Your father left for Japan to study, and I stayed behind with you and your *halmeoni*. I was young, so young and scared. Months went by with no word from him. I was afraid he wasn't coming back. I was afraid I wouldn't be able to take care of myself in Heung-Nam, so I wanted to leave to make a better life. Your *halmeoni* convinced me to leave you because it would be better for her to take care of you than for me as a single woman."

Shang Ik turned away from her and marched off, shaking his head in disbelief. His heart raced as he looked for a place to escape her words. *It's not true. This can't be true. I don't understand this. It doesn't make any sense. Appa never said anything. He never said a word.*

Eomma-Azumma lunged for him, forcing him to turn around and face her through the tears that fell freely from both their faces. "I only agreed to it because I was young and afraid. I never wanted to leave you, but I didn't know what else to do. By the time I left for the South, it was too dangerous to return. Shang Ik, you must believe me. When your father and I saw each other again in Seoul many years later, we agreed that we would tell you who I was. But we wanted to introduce you to me slowly so you wouldn't be frightened."

Shang Ik stopped struggling, allowing her words to wash over him like summer rain. He knew it was true, every single bit of it. He sank to the ground, pulling his knees up to his chest and hanging his head. His heart hurt because it was beating so fast.

She sank into the dirt next to him and lifted his head. "My son, my boy. I never wanted to leave you. I have wanted you, hoped for you, and cried for you for so many years. When your father died, I knew the war was coming. I knew they would implicate me with him because we were once married. And I knew you were in danger. So I told you to leave."

She began to weep, crying with bitterness of soul and a lifetime of regret.

"I knew. I just knew I was being punished for leaving you as a baby and lying to you all that time. That is why I didn't begrudge your *uibus-eomi*'s time with you. She was your *eomma*, and I was happy just to be your *eomma-azumma*. But when the war came and you ran away, I thought you were dead. Oh, I thought you were dead." She buried her head in her hands and wept like a small child.

Shang Ik shook his head in disbelief. *She was my eomma. She was my eomma all along*. She was right there, and he hadn't known it. She wept, rocking herself almost as if attempting to soothe her own wounds.

Shang Ik watched her for a moment, his own heart breaking. *How hard must it have been for her to be young and alone. To leave me behind and then to lose me again after we found each other. Halmeoni had me. Appa had me. And Uibus-Eomi. But she had no one. She's been alone all this time.*

Without hesitation, he pulled her into his chest in an embrace, allowing her to release the anguish of her soul as they sat in the dust and dirt of that courtyard. As he did, he stroked her head, realizing for the first time that he was stroking his *eomma. His eomma.* His heart erupted into flutters of gratitude and joy at the realization that not only did he have a mother but also he had had one all along, and here he was holding her in his arms.

After a few moments of silent sobbing, Shang Ik pulled her off him, compelled by a sudden memory. "*Eomma,* what happened to you? Soon-Ja said you were taken and shot! How did you survive? Where have you been all this time?"

She sat up, her breath shaky and labored. Wiping her eyes, she shook her head and took her time to answer, as if collecting memories that she had hidden away in the dust and cobwebs of her soul. "Shang Ik, my son, it was such a terrible time. Soon after I sent you off, a pounding on my door woke me up. One of my neighbors told the communist military that your father worked for the government. There were rumors about us, allegations we tried to shield you from. But I suspect that many people knew your father and I were once married. Once the communists came, they traded the information for favors or pardon. I don't know."

Shang Ik furrowed his brow and nodded.

"The North Korean soldiers came into my home. They took me and dragged me through the streets until we came to their central base of command." She paused here and slowly shook her head, as if the memory was difficult to say out loud.

Shang Ik took her hand and waited.

After a moment, she continued. "They lined me up with others—some I recognized from town and a few I didn't. We all started to plead with them, but no one would listen. I knew then I was going to die. Your father's friend, Mr. Lee, do you remember him?"

Shang Ik nodded.

"He was there. He took the weapon to execute me. When I saw him, I started pleading. I hoped I could change his mind. But he came to me and slapped me."

Shang Ik shook his head and grimaced at the thought.

"But then, when he came to pick me up from the ground, he whispered in my ear. He said, 'I am assigned to execute you. But I will shoot you with a blank. So you fall, pretend to be dead, and come to my house at night.'"

Shang Ik's eyes widened. He pulled back in shock. "Mr. Lee was a double agent?"

His mother nodded. "Yes. He was working with the North Koreans but getting information to help the South. I suppose that is why he wanted to meet with your father so much, to learn about the plans the South and the Americans were making and to tell him what the North Koreans would do next. Mr. Lee and your father became friends. Mr. Lee saved my life."

Shang Ik's eyes opened wide. He couldn't believe it. "Then what happened, *Eomma*. Where did you go?"

"I did as he told me. When he fired the blank, I fell to the ground. I lay in that ditch for hours with the many dead bodies. I was afraid to move. But once nightfall came, I crawled out of the ditch. Then I went to his house. He had dug a hole under his living room that he had covered with wooden planks. I hid there in that hole for three months. I survived in that hole until General McArthur's army came and retook Seoul."

Shang Ik ran his hands through his hair, reeling. *"Eomma,* you were in Seoul the whole time Soon-Ja and I thought you were dead? We were here. We didn't leave until after McArthur recaptured the city."

His mother nodded sadly. "Yes, I was there, hidden. As soon as Mr. Lee thought it was safe for me to leave, I went looking for you and your sister. I went to her house, but you had already gone."

Shang Ik shook his head, saddened. *She was there the whole time. We were so close to each other, and we kept missing each other. Even now, if I had waited a week or come too soon or not at all, I would have missed her here. Or what if she would have found us and left with us for Uh-Jung-Geh? She might have died with Soon-Ja.*

His mother continued. "After that, I went to the city of Pusan, near the very end of the South. I tried to make a life for myself there. The whole time, I thought you were dead. I thought you were dead." She buried her head in her hands and began to weep.

Shang Ik lay his head against the water pump, his own tears threatening to overtake him. "*Eomma*, I thought you were dead too. In fact, I thought you were dead my whole life. I thought I didn't have a mother. But look at us. We have found each other. We have each other now after all this time."

She shook her head, overwhelmed, and continued to weep, allowing her tears to soothe her soul. Shang Ik held his mother in his arms as he leaned his head against the pump, his own cheeks dripping wet from tears of joy.

As he sat against the pump, a phrase came to his mind, jumping into his subconscious uninvited. The suddenness of it reminded him of hearing the voice on the mountaintop on his way to Mang-Ri. He didn't recognize it then, but it felt familiar now. He even recognized the exact passage it was. *Isaiah. Somewhere in Isaiah.* Shang Ik allowed the words of the phrase to ruminate in his mind as he sat there, holding his mother in his arms and squeezing her in toward himself as if to imprint her onto his heart.

Behold, I will do a new thing. Now it shall spring forth; Shall you not know it? I will even make a road in the wilderness and rivers in the desert.

Last Stop

Shang Ik and his mother sat together on the ground for a long time. Mother and son took considerable time to share each other's harrowing experiences that led them to this point. She shared with him about her work and how she built her business. He told her how he heard from relatives that Duk-Soo had been found and well cared for by another member of Jong Pil's household. Soon twilight settled over the courtyard. It was dark by the time Shang Ik returned to the jeep.

The chaplain, wanting to let the boy have his moment, had leaned back in his seat and was fast asleep when Shang Ik hopped into the passenger side. The sound of the door slamming jarred the chaplain awake. He sat up and looked around, rubbing his face. Shang Ik leaned back against the headrest, exhausted.

"How was it, Moon?"

Shang Ik did not hear him. He simply sat in the jeep's passenger side, silent. He looked out the window at the sight of two boys chasing each other in the dusk. They laughed and ran, almost as if unaware that just outside their little neighborhood were the remnants of devastation and loss, a loss they would hopefully never know. They chased each other, carefree and alive, rounding the corner until Shang Ik couldn't see them anymore.

He sighed deeply. Then he pitched forward and buried his head in his hands. Sobs poured out of his soul like a torrent. His throat was tight, and his chest was burning, but he couldn't stop crying. He sucked air into his lungs in intermittent breaths, but still the tears would not stop. Chaplain Vajda reached over, pulled Shang Ik into his chest, and held the boy as he cried.

After a few minutes, the tears subsided, and he was able to speak. "Chapy, alive. She alive whole time. Whole time I thought she dead. I thought she tortured and killed and I was alone. And she alive. What the reason? Why now when I leave for America?"

The chaplain tilted his head back, leaning against his headrest with his eyes closed. He kept his hand on Shang Ik's shoulder, deep in thought, while Shang Ik stared at him, waiting desperately for an answer to his question.

"Moon, I don't know why you found her now. But I do know, from everything you've told me, that there was no way for either of you to communicate with each other. She wouldn't have known where you were at all. Nor you her. And what are the odds that you both return to Seoul within a week of each other? In my mind, finding each other like this was a gift. It so easily could have never happened."

Shang Ik wiped his eyes, nodding as he tried to settle his breathing. "But how am I going to tell her that I am soon going away to America?"

The chaplain leaned in closer to Shang Ik and spoke urgently. "Moon, you found her. And now that I'm going back to America, you can stay with her until your visa clears and you are ready to go. It will take months for that visa to clear. That's months with your mother you wouldn't have had otherwise. Think of it that way."

Shang Ik nodded. He had spent the past hours with his mother, rehashing the last three years. He told her about Soon-Ja and Soon-Ja's baby, and she wept. Shang Ik did not elaborate about his time in Mang-Ri with Soon-Ja's in-laws. It was his most bitter time, and he wanted to spare her details of his suffering. He also did not tell her about rummaging through the garbage dump, only that he made his way to the air force base and met the chaplain and that now he was doing fine.

The son also kept from his mother the small detail that he was about to go to America to study to become a Christian missionary. After hours of catching up, weeping and laughing, they were both tired. His mother did not want to let him go, but he promised her he would return the next day and he would come to stay with her as soon as possible.

When the chaplain and Shang Ik returned to the base late that evening, they sat together for some time in the chaplain's office. At first they were quiet, absorbing the day.

After a while, Chaplain Vajda cleared his throat, shifted in his chair, and turned to his assistant. "Moon, my tour is up, and it is time for me to return to America. You will be allowed to stay here at the base until your visa clears. I've made arrangements for that. You can have your room and your meals and work for some other chaplain or officer."

But Shang Ik shook his head. "No, Chapy, thank you. Thank you everything you done for me. But I live with *Eomma*. I spend much time with her before leave."

Chaplain Vajda nodded and smiled. "I figured you would say that. When you and your mother are ready, you're free to go."

Both stood, and the officer grasped Shang Ik on the shoulders. "Get some rest, Moon. Tomorrow we'll sort out the details."

Shang Ik turned to leave but stopped at the door. "Chapy?"

Vajda lowered his hands from rubbing his eyes. "Yes, Moon?"

Shang Ik hesitated, not wanting to embarrass himself by crying again. "Thank you. Thank you for taking me Seoul. Thank you teaching me English and taking good care for me. Thank you for teaching me about your God and for everything you do. I forever grateful to you." He left without waiting for a response.

Chaplain Vajda stood alone, waiting until the boy closed the door before collapsing onto his chair and bringing his hands back up to his eyes.

For the rest of that week, the chaplain and Shang Ik were mostly silent around each other. They went to mess hall together every day, as they were accustomed, and Shang Ik helped his chaplain prepare whatever was needed for the chapel. Few words were spoken between them. A bond had developed that went beyond words.

One week later, Chaplain Vajda boarded a flight to America. Their goodbye was brief. A light hug and a pat on the back was all that passed between them. But Shang Ik stayed on the tarmac until the plane was undetectable in the sky, fingering the little cross pin his Chapy had given him.

Shang Ik returned to visit his *eomma* often. He was relieved to discover that his mother was blessed to have done well while she was in the southern part of Korea. She had opened a restaurant in Pusan and made a reasonable amount of money. But now she decided to stay in Seoul. With the money she made from her restaurant, she decided to buy a house where she and Shang Ik would live together.

Shang Ik moved in with her soon after Chaplain Vajda left. He couldn't bear to stay in the base long after that. His year and a half at the base had given him more than he could have imagined or wished for. He had made friends with the airmen and officers, and all gave him hugs and good wishes when he left. He walked into that base a starving orphan, but he left with an education, a future, and faith, perhaps the most precious gift to what was once a desperate and hopeless boy.

The day he finally moved in with *Eomma* at their new home, they were sitting together in the kitchen, unpacking some utensils and bowls she brought with her from her old restaurant. Working together quietly in the kitchen, Shang Ik knew it was time for him to come clean about his future plans.

"*Eomma*, something wonderful happened when I was at the base. I was given the opportunity to go to America to study. Chaplain Vajda set it up for me. I have a scholarship, and I've been accepted to a college."

Chang-Nyo's eyes widened at the news, and she sank back in her chair. "Well, that is amazing. That's wonderful news for you, Shang Ik, but what are you going to study?"

Shang Ik hesitated, knowing what her response would be. "I'm going to study to become a Christian missionary."

Chang-Nyo furrowed her brow and shook her head, standing up from her chair.

Shang Ik began speaking quickly. "*Eomma*, I understand that we never knew much about Christians. They are strange people. That's all we knew. But the Christians at the base were the kindest people I ever met. They cared for me and treated me well. They provided for me. They took me in when I was starving and sleeping on the ground in a tent."

His mother walked over to the small kitchen window. A light breeze lifted the blue curtain she had just hung. She looked out into the garden with her hands folded across her chest. After a few moments, she sighed and bowed her head. Shang Ik stood softly and came to stand next to her.

Putting his hand on her shoulder, he turned her to face him. "*Eomma*, in the mountains, running for my life, I thought I was all alone. I thought I had no one left in the world. And when I was the most alone, that is when I felt God with me. I remembered something I had heard from my friend Whan Soo's pastor, something his God said: 'Lo, I am with you always.'

"They say He is the God of the whole universe, who made all things. And I felt Him with me! Imagine what that was like! To know that the God who is the only God was with me when I needed Him most. I didn't know Him, but I felt Him, *Eomma*. I know He inspired people like Chapy to take care of others and to feed the hungry and the poor. I want to learn more about Him because it was through Him that I received kindness when I needed it most, from people whom I least expected. That's what I want to learn, and that's what I want to share with our people here in Korea."

In silence, Chang-Nyo turned her gaze back out the window, the sadness in her eyes bringing pain to Shang Ik's soul.

"*Eomma*, don't worry about me. I know this is not what you wanted for me. I know you wanted me to be a doctor or lawyer. But this is the only thing I want to do."

His mother shook her head and turned to her son. "Shang Ik, I am not sad because of what you want to do. I am sad because of how much time has passed between us. Your grandmother took you away from me when you were only a toddler. All along you were told I was dead. Many moons later, when your father and I accidently ran into each other on a busy street of Seoul, we dreamed to put our family together again. But then the cruel Korean War erupted, and the rest is history! For so long I thought you were dead. But you are living. I know I have no more claim over you. You must go. Go. Follow your dreams and your God. I won't stand in your way."

Shang Ik exhaled, unaware of how much having her blessing meant to him. He put his arm around her, and she leaned her head against his chest, placing her hand over his heart.

They enjoyed every day together, making up for lost time. Each day was intentional and directed toward the furthering of their relationship. They had many long conversations during which Shang Ik would share his deepest thoughts with *Eomma*, cluing her into his own internal struggle with his new faith and the customs he was raised in. They shared their fears, dreams, and experiences. They intentionally did not rehash the more negative moments of the last few years. Everything that passed between them was purposed toward tethering their souls together in preparation for the moment when they would be separated yet again.

Six months later, Shang Ik's visa was approved, and in January 1955, Shang Ik, his mother, and many of their friends headed to the Seoul Airport, where an airplane was waiting to take him to America.

At eighteen years of age, Shang Ik did not want to show how nervous he was about going on an airplane for the first time. Besides he didn't want his *eomma* to worry more than she had to. As it was, she was holding back tears. Shang Ik tried to keep her spirits light by promising to write every day and pretending to be excited about going to America.

Chang-Nyo looked at the large propeller airplane with the words "Pan American Airway" on it and clenched her fists to suppress her tears. She gave Shang Ik two bouquets of flowers, one from her and one from his friends at the air force base.

"These flowers are for luck, Shang Ik. I know you don't believe in luck anymore, but you'll take them for your *eomma*, right?" she said as she placed the bouquets in his hand.

Shang Ik silently nodded and took the flowers. His face darkened as he saw people beginning to board the plane. His time was up.

Eomma snapped her fingers. "I remember! Mrs. Chen and I bought this together. It's for you. For you to take with you to school and to remember your home here." She pulled out a small camera, one of the brand-new models. Holding it up to her face, she tried to smile. "Hold up your flowers, Shang Ik. Smile for the picture."

Shang Ik held the flowers and did his best to smile. She took the photo and then placed the camera around his neck by the strap.

As she adjusted his coat and smoothed out his hair, her hands trembled. "Promise that you will send to me many pictures from America!"

Shang Ik reached up and grabbed his mother's hand, holding it in his for the last time. He leaned his head in, touching his forehead to hers. They stayed that way for a moment.

Then she took a deep breath. "Go," she whispered. "This is your time. Go."

She gently pushed him, and he silently turned and walked toward the plane. Holding tightly to the bouquets of flowers allowed him to hide the quiver in his mouth as he turned away from his mother. The all too familiar terror of not knowing if he would ever see her again settled in the pit of his stomach as he boarded the airplane.

Finding his seat, he looked out the window. She was still there, clutching her coat closed to the crisp January air. The wind blew her hair wildly around her face. Shang Ik leaned into the cold airplane window, burning the vision of her into his memory. His *eomma*, alive and well, healthy and taken care of, that was how he always wanted to remember her.

There was a jolt, and the propellers began their buzzing rotation. The sound was deafening. Out the window, the wind from the propellers sent his mother and the rest of the bystanders fleeing from their spot on the tarmac.

The plane began to taxi toward the runway where they would begin their takeoff. As the aircraft rose into the clouds, Shang Ik kept his gaze toward the window until Korea was nothing but a memory.

A Korean in Kansas

In 1953 it took three days to reach Kansas City in America and another day for the ringing in Shang Ik's ear to subside. As if it weren't difficult enough to understand and be understood in America, he now had to shout at everyone he met because his eardrums still pulsed from the many hours spent with the buzz of the propeller plane.

After landing in Kansas City and retrieving his luggage, Shang Ik nervously scanned the crowd at baggage claim. It was obvious that he was the only foreigner, perhaps the only Korean, in the entire state of Kansas. Signs and instructions were hard to comprehend, and directions to local transportation were very confusing to the cultural novice. After several minutes of confused wandering, he saw a tired-looking man holding a sign with his name on it.

Approaching the man shyly, Shang Ik waved his hand. "Hello! I Shang Ik Moon!"

The man smiled warmly and clapped Shang Ik on the back. "Why hello there! How are you? Welcome! Welcome to America! You must be freezing and exhausted. It must be such a long flight all the way from halfway around the world. Well, come on. Come on. The car's waiting."

He turned quickly as Shang Ik nodded, although he did not understand fully what the man had said. Shang Ik struggled with his bags as he followed the man outside to a yellow taxicab.

The man placed Shang Ik's luggage in the trunk and pointed to the car's backdoor. "Have a seat right here. Don't dawdle. Let's get you over to the college."

Shang Ik obeyed the man and settled into the back seat. "Sir, you know who I meet at college? I have letter."

"Well, I'll tell you that I don't have any clue who you're supposed to meet at the school, but once we get there, I'll help you out to get settled as best I can. Korea, huh? I had a cousin who fought over there. But I suppose you don't want to talk about that."

Shang Ik didn't, but he simply smiled and looked out the window. The driver continued asking questions that Shang Ik couldn't answer with his insufficient English.

Vast open prairies and wheat fields with wind-swept snow stretched for miles. The small homes and farmhouses looked welcoming. Once they got into the town's perimeter, clean streets and small shops gave Shang Ik a feeling of calm. From the entry to Winfield, it was only a short way to Saint John's College.

Saint John's stood regal yet quaint looking in the center of the town. The limestone building tucked beneath snow-covered maple trees reminded Shang Ik of magazine photos he had seen of America. It was the picture of American life. He exited the taxi as the man placed his bags on the sidewalk. The new student took a moment to calm himself before he continued toward the office. *It's OK. You can do this. This is what you and Chapy prepared for. Just go inside and ask for help.*

Once he managed to get his luggage through the office door, Shang Ik approached the front desk. It turned out his conversational English was barely understandable. Or perhaps their Kansas accents weren't understandable to him. Either way it was a much tougher conversation than he anticipated. At least the woman at the reception desk was kind and patient. The college was eagerly anticipating the new student from Korea. Eventually he was able to ascertain the information he needed about where to go and with whom to speak.

Dr. Wente, the academic dean, personally came to welcome their foreign student and to escort him to his room. Dr. Wente shook Shang Ik's hand firmly and gave him a detailed description of the campus, little of which Shang Ik understood. He was then dropped off in his room with a campus map and class guide.

Within an hour Shang Ik settled into his room on campus. Thoughts swirled like a tornado in his mind. *What am I doing here? I must have been crazy to think I had any chance of succeeding in a college, let alone one so far away from home and so foreign.*

Shang Ik's first week in school was a whirlwind. His fellow students were quite pleasant and helpful. One of them was always willing to offer directions to the next class or to share his notes on a lecture. The kind gestures from his peers and the faculty did aid him in the transition to college life. However, by the end of the first week, despite the buffer of their kindness, he found that the language barrier alone was enough to make him desperate for Korea.

Shang Ik's high school education only lasted until he had to flee South Korea in the dark of night. He spent the rest of his school years in survival mode, fleeing gunfire or struggling for basic survival. His academic knowledge had been sufficient for the American military base in Korea, and his daily talks with Chapy had given him what he thought was satisfactory conversational English.

However, conversational English was not sufficient to understand textbooks and class lectures. No matter where he went, his pocket dictionary was always with him. Mastering the content of every assignment took him three times as long as it did a native English speaker. All that week he burned the midnight oil, sometimes only finishing his assignments in the early hours of the morning.

As a pre-seminary student, he was required to master three languages in addition to his other coursework: Greek, German, and Latin. The burden of learning three languages while he was still trying to grasp English was proving to be too much. After a couple of weeks of intense struggle, Shang Ik made an appointment to speak to Dr. Wente. The dean was a blessing to his charges. He made time for any student who wanted to speak to him, in spite of his stature and busy schedule.

When he saw Shang Ik sitting outside his office, looking bone-weary and anxious, he was concerned. The dean pushed aside the papers he was grading and ushered Shang Ik into his office.

"Dr. Wente," Shang Ik began, his arms loaded with textbooks and notes that he struggled to balance as he sat in the chair. "I cannot do this anymore."

"All right. Have a seat and calm down. What's the problem?"

"I confused with languages. I don't understand. And I can't do work if I don't understand!"

Dr. Wente nodded and allowed Shang Ik to spill out his feelings and frustrations.

"Thank you for opportunity to come to college. But I think I quit."

"Whoa! Hold on a moment, Shang Ik." Dr. Wente sat forward with a concerned look on his face. "What about if we got you a tutor? Would that help? Some private tutoring during your free time. A faculty intern is a whiz at Greek. He is sensitive and patient. I am sure I can get him to help you."

Shang Ik sighed and shrugged his shoulders. "I don't know, Doctor. I suppose tutor might help."

Dr. Wente stood up and buzzed his secretary. "Mary Ann? Get me Ralph Bohlmann."

Ralph Bohlmann came into Shang Ik's life like a heroic knight. The resident instructor in internship tutored his new Korean friend in Greek, German, and Latin and helped him with the other subjects he was taking. Ralph approached teaching Shang Ik with a commitment and determination that said to Shang Ik, "We care. You are valuable."

In spite of Ralph's best efforts, Shang Ik got halfway through the first semester and knew he was still too far behind. His grades and papers weren't reflecting where he believed he should be. Discouraged, he returned to Dr. Wente's office.

"Dr. Wente, thank you for sending Ralph Bohlmann to me. I not making progress. I struggle every day. Always behind. If I not understand one word in a sentence, I lose the entire sentence! I really feel I should quit and go home."

Dr. Wente was silent. He observed Shang Ik for a moment. Then he slowly leaned in and challenged the boy. "You know, Shang Ik, your teachers tell me you are improving. They tell me you've made progress. Why not give it another week? Just one more week and see how you feel."

Shang Ik shook his head, not convinced. However, he agreed, trying harder in that week than he ever had before. He stayed awake until two or three in the morning, but the effort did not make him feel any less behind. By the end of the week, he returned to Dr. Wente, feeling defeated.

"Dr. Wente, I try, but I'm exhausted. And it didn't make difference. I'm still so behind."

Dr. Wente got out from behind his desk and put his arm around Shang Ik. "Shang Ik! It would be such a shame to quit now with more than half the semester behind you. Why don't you finish this semester and see how you feel about it? It's a shame to lose all the work you've done and quit without seeing how the semester will end, don't you think?"

Shang Ik shrugged. The truth was that he was too tired to argue.

"After the semester ends, if you still feel you are not making it, then we will make a decision. But let's not make a decision now. Meanwhile, go and just do your best. That is all I ask."

He gently pushed Shang Ik out the door. Shang Ik left, wondering why he should keep trying at something that was so obviously a failure.

He kept his word to Dr. Wente to finish the semester. He met with Ralph Bohlmann nearly every day and continued progressing, wanting desperately to reach the finish line. At the close of the first semester, he went to Dr. Wente's office to assess his grades.

Dr. Wente greeted him with a warm smile and excitement in his voice. He waved Shang Ik in and slammed his palm on the desk. "You've done it! I have grades from all your professors. Would you believe that you have passed many of your classes with As and Bs?"

Shang Ik's eyes widened, and he sat back in his chair. "No, I didn't know that, Dr. Wente. I didn't realize I was doing that well."

"You see, Shang Ik, sometimes it's necessary to hold on through the hard times. They will get better."

Shang Ik nodded, surprised he hadn't grasped that concept with all the hard times he had held on through in his life.

Dr. Wente leaned down and looked him in the eye. "You made it through the semester. If you go back home to Korea, how are you going to explain why you went back so soon? You're not going to quit now, are you?"

Shang Ik smiled and nodded, determined to begin the next semester as strongly as he had finished this one. Many times throughout the second semester, he wanted to quit, as the academic requirements became harder and harder. But he would go see Dr. Wente, who would always give him a reason to hold on a little longer.

"You've finished the second semester. Finish at least this academic year."

"You've got one year under your belt. What's one more?"

Shang Ik's first year at Saint John's flew by, and he began to enjoy his life in Kansas. He made friends with students and teachers who wanted to help him. Soon he stopped thinking about quitting. By his second year, he began to grasp the "feeling of the language." He especially enjoyed the small-town campus life.

One of the most influential aspects of his time at Saint John's was the emphasis on intellectual honesty. Shang Ik had heard that America was a free country, where you were able to think and express what you wanted. It was not just in word but in deed. He saw he was able to express his opinion without being penalized or looked down upon.

In America, you could agree to disagree, and disagreeing was not wrong. This was not how Shang Ik was taught. In Korea, to disagree with a professor was a sign of great disrespect and dishonor. The student's job was to absorb the great wisdom the professor would give and not dare challenge it.

But at Saint John's, Shang Ik learned the value of his own opinions, thoughts, and feelings. For the first time, he was able to open up his own soul and mind and say what he thought without worrying that the professor would punish him. In the context of his culture, you are obligated to be right and to honor your elders and agree with them, even if you know they are wrong. Shang Ik spent much of his time at Saint John's contemplating the Confucian ideology that he had been raised in, where he was taught to know his place and to act his status and role.

In America, he was learning that being subordinate and respectful was valued, but the truth was dearer. He learned to not be a passive learner. He grew to view it as a more mature version of freedom and came to value the self-determination required to own his own opinions and feelings.

After two years, Shang Ik graduated from Saint John's as the valedictorian of his class and went on to Concordia Senior College in Fort Wayne, Indiana. The college had been established for the young men studying to be pastors to complete their last two years of college. They began their studies at one of a network of ten Concordia Colleges situated around the United States. After this, they would come together at Fort Wayne to complete the last two years in preparation for the seminary education.

Shang Ik's time at the Senior College kindled in him an even greater fascination with American culture. Thanks to the Japanese subjugation of Korea, he grew up sheltered from other world cultures. As a result, he could not resist taking advantage of his access to American education to study more about the world he had been so sheltered from.

His experience in Fort Wayne was made more perfect when Dr. Wente transferred from Saint John's and became academic dean at Concordia Senior College. Shang Ik was free to drop into his office at any time, for any situation. It was at Concordia Senior College that he chose sociology and anthropology as his majors, wanting to better understand the culture shock he experienced coming from an Eastern to a Western culture. He wanted to soak in as much from other cultures as he could before he returned to Korea as a missionary.

After two years, he left Concordia Senior College with a bachelor's in sociology. Shang Ik was then ready to focus on his seminary studies, eager to learn what was necessary for him to return to Korea as a missionary to his people. He entered Concordia Seminary in Saint Louis in 1959, graduating in 1963 with a master of divinity degree.

Seminary for Shang Ik proved to be a cathartic experience. It was a time of spiritual formation. It opened for him the hidden nature of the God in whom he had come to believe. For some students, the seminary was a place to learn how to prove God's existence and to flex their theological muscle. For Shang Ik, theology simply proved his own experience. As he stood before the class one day, sharing his view on God's existence, he grew into the opinion that his times of heartache were, in fact, a gift. It was a soothing blessing to come to that conclusion of his experiences, in spite of the scars they still left on his heart.

With a surge of boldness that was new for him, Shang Ik stood before one of his theology classes on assignment, giving his analysis of theology based on his personal experiences. "For me, I cannot prove that

God exists based only on quoting theories like Thomas Aquinas. But I can make the assertion. I know that God is alive and that He provides for us. It has been proven to me. I cannot prove it to you, but it has been proven to me. The Holy Spirit, whom I did not know at the time, assured me of God's presence when I thought I was alone, surrounded by death on a mountain in Korea. At that point, I remembered a phrase from a Christian friend, something I did not know was from God's Word: 'I am with you always.' That word spoke to my desperate condition. From that moment, I believed."

Korea still burned in Shang Ik's heart, but now he wanted to share Korea with his friends and the people who had become his family. Shang Ik often shared his convictions with his seminary roommate, John Hodde, who showed a great interest in foreign mission work.

"How about Korea? We can go there together as a team, right?" Shang Ik asked John, making plans with youthful naiveté and exuberance.

John eagerly agreed. Both young men were burning with a passion to spread their earnest convictions around the world.

When both men graduated in the class of 1963, John was commissioned to Korea as a missionary while Shang Ik went on to additional graduate study in sociology.

Still infatuated with the differences in culture and society and believing that the study of people would be necessary for him to truly benefit his Korean mission, Shang Ik applied for admission to Washington University in Saint Louis. After two more years of study, he received a master's degree in sociology. He then went on to Saint Louis University, where, after arduous effort, he received his PhD in sociology.

After the ceremony conferring his degree, Shang Ik took some time alone in his room, contemplating the measure of his years of hard work. He chuckled. *I guess Eomma was right. I did become a doctor. Doctor Shang Ik Moon.* He stood in front of his mirror, feeling taller and wiser than he had that morning. *It's time for me to go back. Eomma's letters say that things in Korea have gotten much better. I've studied and learned everything I can. It's time for me to go home.*

Shang Ik soon contacted his church's mission department and associates in Korea. Writing a formal letter, he detailed his desire to be commissioned to his home country. *I feel I have learned everything I need to know about American culture and theology, and I am excited to return to my home and begin an important and much-needed ministry in that part of the world.*

He eagerly anticipated the response from the mission board, telling him his call to Korea had been approved. When it arrived, he casually tore it open, preparing to skim the letters for the exact dates he should make his preparations. His eyes fell on a line that he had to read twice before he understood its meaning. *Your request for assignment to Korea has been rejected.*

Shang Ik blinked twice and then read the letter from the beginning. The Lutheran Church of Korea had established its own seminary in Korea and was already training graduates who were being placed in ministry. It would not be fair to call someone from outside the country, even someone born in Korea, to take the place of one of the indigenous seminarians. The church's Board for Missions had determined that there was no need for Shang Ik to return to Korea.

Shang Ik dropped the letter and sank into a chair, stunned. *I'm not going home.*

Hometown Mission

Shang Ik was heartbroken. He could feel everything that Chaplain Vajda had done for him vanish into thin air. Ashamed, he kept his head down when he interacted with his peers, but he began to hear rumors that the church leaders thought Shang Ik was out of touch with Korean society because he left when he was so young and a lot had changed since the communist invasion.

He felt dejected by the revelation that they did not consider him useful and began to wonder what else he could do with all the time and effort he had put into his schooling. Returning to Korea had always been the plan. He hadn't considered any other options.

While still in Saint Louis, Shang Ik met a young man at Concordia Seminary by the name of Charles Lentner, who would become his close friend. Korea intrigued Charles

Lentner, and he wanted to learn everything he could about Korea and its culture. Charles had a sister, Sharon Louise, who was also in Saint Louis, studying to become a nurse. Her dream had been to serve as an overseas missionary nurse.

The friendships of Charles and Sharon Louise somewhat assuaged Shang Ik's bitter disappointment. Sharon and Shang Ik would often meet for coffee at a local diner that many of the college students frequented.

"I just don't understand it," Shang Ik said as he stirred his cup of coffee.

Sharon took a bite of her pie and stared out the window, wanting to season her response with compassion for his feelings. "Shang Ik, I don't think their rejection had anything to do with you. It isn't anything you did or didn't do. It just makes more sense for them and their needs. It isn't personal, youknow?"

"How could it not be personal, Sharon? I'm Korean. It's my home. Going back there was always my plan. It was my idea, or at least I thought it was. How could they not think I'm good enough?"

Sharon placed her hands on his and smiled sympathetically. "Of course you're good enough. Being good enough isn't the question. You'll find what you're supposed to do, Shang Ik. I'm certain of it."

Shang Ik smiled, returning the squeeze of her hand, holding it a little longer than usual. Shang Ik and Sharon had a few more heartfelt conversations after that, until soon they stopped talking about Korea and started discussing other things.

On June 11, 1966, Shang Ik and Sharon Louise were married.

Upon graduation from seminary, the church called Shang Ik's new brother-in-law, now

Reverend Charles Lentner, to be a missionary. Adding insult to injury, the church assigned Charles to Korea.

It took time for Shang Ik to overcome the bitter disappointment of not returning to his home as a missionary, but with Sharon's help, Shang Ik had come to understand that planning for his life was pointless. He certainly hadn't planned to meet Chaplain Vajda or to ever come to America, and yet here he was. He had given up on expectations and resigned himself to the reality that he couldn't plan the rest of his life.

He saw Charles off to Korea with joy in his heart while he settled into his new life with Sharon.

As happy as those first few years were, no amount of marital bliss could fully erase the sting of being rejected from what he felt was his life's calling. *My seminary roommate is in Korea, and my brother-in-law is now in*

Korea. We shared that dream, and we were supposed to do it together. Now they're there, and I'm here. I'm the Korean! What am I supposed to do with my life? How will I know when I find it?

Having stayed in Saint Louis to finish his doctorate, Shang Ik was ready to get to work. It was 1970, and Shang Ik received a call to teach at Concordia Senior College in Fort Wayne, Indiana. The school's trustees had heard he would not be returning to Korea, so they offered the new Dr. Moon the opportunity to teach sociology at his alma mater. With his master of divinity degree and his doctorate in the social sciences, he had exactly what was required to teach pre-seminary students.

At first, this opportunity consoled Shang Ik. He loved teaching. Even so, from time to time, the sting of rejection would surface. He still believed his true calling was as a missionary.

As he spent time in class with the students, they would raise questions about cultural differences and the implications of this for sharing the gospel. He began to take time during class to address these missiological issues. The more time he spent with his students, the more his mind began to open to the possibility that this was where he was supposed to be.

His perspective on staying in America began to alter with each eager young mind that peppered him with questions. These new students were so eager and so green, yet they were so full of passion to do good in the world. They saw Shang Ik as someone who had a world of experience and insight to prepare and equip them. They looked to him to help them grasp the concept of life and culture outside of Middle America.

His reputation soon began to spread outside of the school. He began to receive invitations to go to different churches to share his story at mission festivals. He and Sharon would pack up the car and travel all around the countryside. He would preach in the mornings, and in the afternoons, he would share his personal story and teach a Bible study on the church's mission to hundreds of people. He gave testimony about Chaplain Vajda's efforts to minister under the adverse circumstances of war and poverty. He found himself preaching and teaching pastors all over Indiana.

Reliving the horrors he had faced in Korea was difficult, but he found comfort in the respect given to him by those attending the mission gatherings. He had been given a mission to open the hearts of thousands of people to the importance of spreading the gospel all over the globe. What's more, he stood before them as a living witness to the importance of bringing the good news of God's love to people in distant lands. People understood the importance of reaching out to other nations, especially when he shared the story of an American air force chaplain who had made Jesus's love known to a destitute Korean immigrant.

He could challenge American Christians to move outside of their own comforts and to see the mission field right in front of them. They didn't need to travel to Korea, Nigeria, or Argentina. Koreans, Argentinians, and Nigerians were coming to America by the thousands. Shang Ik talked about the opportunities to expand international mission efforts at home without having to make as many sacrifices as earlier missionaries made by going overseas. Many flocked to America like he did, in search of greater opportunity. The ground in America was fertile for mission outreach because the mission field had come to the country's backyard.

Shang Ik spent six years as a professor of sociology at Concordia Senior College, gaining a reputation in the area as a preacher as well as a teacher. One day in 1976, Shang Ik received a telephone call from Dr. Charles Manske, who had just been appointed the president of Christ College in Irvine, California. Dr. Manske was interviewing potential faculty for the school's start-up. Even the campus was still under construction.

Having heard of Shang Ik through mutual friends, he was very interested in having a Korean professor come to his new college and join him in what he called a "Great Commission College" as the academic dean and a professor of sociology.

"Dr. Moon, we understand you are a scholar with the heart of a missionary. I'd like to tell you about a new college we are beginning here in Irvine, California. We see it as much as a mission as a place of study. It won't be easy to get the school off the ground. We need teachers who know how to sacrifice and work hard and love seeing people come alive when they hear the gospel."

After speaking with Dr. Manske, Shang Ik learned that the primary focus of this school would be training for pastors and missionaries.

"What do you think? It sounds like a wonderful opportunity, but it would mean a big change for our family. The kids have school and their friends. It would mean uprooting them."

Shang Ik and Sharon discussed the opportunity as they prepared for bed one night. Sharon sighed deeply while she brushed her hair, pausing to give a good response as she always had. "Well, Moon, you know you've been wanting a change. It couldn't hurt to head out to California to see what you would be dealing with."

They agreed he would go to California to assess the school and the possibility of joining their faculty. Once there, he realized what a wonderful opportunity the school and the surrounding area presented. The ethnic communities in the Los Angeles area were vast and diverse, and a few Korean churches had already been started, although none was Lutheran.

Shang Ik felt instantly that this was where he needed to be. He returned home full of more excitement and expectation than he had felt in a long time. Soon he and Sharon and their three children, Sharine, Sarah, and Paul, moved to Irvine, California.

Starting a new college was no easy matter. The administrators and professors worked long hours, one doing the work of two. It was a difficult time but in many ways a joyous one. The faculty became close, united behind an effort to create a true mission college.

When he first came to what was then Christ College in 1976, they had only thirty-six students. Shang Ik and the other founding faculty had to recruit students from all the highways and byways with very little to show for it those first few years.

There was talk of closing the school and selling the land from the higher-ups in the Lutheran Mission Board. Two months before the start of their fall semester, representatives came to persuade them to close the school because they didn't have enough students to justify the investment. Shang Ik convinced his fellow founding members that they should keep the school open even if they had only those thirty-six students. They committed to seeing them through four years of their education in pastoral training. By the end of those four years, Christ College Irvine had enrolled two hundred students.

When the school was in the beginning stages and everyone was expecting it to fail—and in fact when their initial enrollment numbers suggested they had failed—Shang Ik had the confidence to encourage his fellow laborers to move forward.

"It's not just a numbers game. It's our effort, and ultimately, we have to trust that God's will is there."

As he became acquainted with the Korean immigrants in greater Los Angeles, he grew more sensitive to their specific needs, rooted in issues he himself had faced. *Time* nicknamed LA the "New Ellis Island," and the number of Korean immigrant churches in LA already surpassed a hundred.

He had met many Korean pastors, but many Korean clergy had suffered as he had. Many had made sacrifices to finish academic requirements in Korea to be ordained. However, not many could meet the qualifications to become part of a denomination in the United States. Shang Ik grew encouraged that his denomination could mobilize resources to meet those needs.

Wanting to maintain their network of Lutheran laborers, as was their tradition, Shang Ik realized he needed to establish a training program to train the Korean pastors in the Los Angeles area in the Lutheran tradition. Shang Ik drew up a proposal to begin a pastoral training program.

The possibilities were endless, and he was ecstatic when he approached Reverend Ken Behnken, the director of missions for the Pacific Southwest District of the LCMS. There was a kindred spirit between Shang Ik and Ken, as they were fellow alumni of Saint John's College. They began the process of getting approval through the different committees of the District Board of Missions to start a Korean language church.

Having to appeal to the Pacific Southwest District mission board reminded him of the last time he had expected a positive answer from a mission board, when they had determined he was not needed in Korea. It was with hesitation that he submitted a proposal for the new church.

The district and the college loved the challenge. The district president, Dr. Arnold Kuntz, and the college president, Dr. Charles Manske, threw their weight behind the proposal. The plan was approved, and Shang Ik was given the go-ahead to begin the program as the director.

In 1988, the first class of the Korean Pastors Colloquy Program began with five students. Their curriculum had been approved by none other than Shang Ik's old tutor at Saint John's College, Ralph Bohlmann, former professor and president of Concordia Seminary, now president of the Lutheran Church Missouri Synod.

In the year 2016, under the guidance and training of Shang Ik, sixty-two new pastors came through the pastoral training program.

Shang Ik, Sharon Louise, and their three children remained in Irvine, where Shang Ik served as vice president for academic affairs and provost. In 1993, the board of regents at Christ College voted to change the name of the school to Concordia University Irvine, making it the tenth campus in the national Concordia University System.

Shang Ik officially retired from his positions as professor of sociology, academic dean, and vice president for academic affairs at Concordia University Irvine in 2002, but he still worked part-time as executive vice president for international relationship, overseeing their sister schools for many years after his retirement. His legacy includes thousands of seminary, theology, and sociology students as well as trained pastors ready to begin their work carrying out the Great Commission around the world.

Epilogue

Now Shang Ik and Sharon stood in the terminal of the Indianapolis International Airport, separated from the runway by a cordoned-off section. There they waited as Sharine, Sarah, and Paul took turns testing the boundaries of the official cord, dipping underneath it whenever their parents weren't looking. Shang Ik took a deep breath, and Sharon squeezed his hand.

"Are you nervous?" she asked, smiling as she leaned into him.

Shang Ik chuckled lightly and put his arm around her. "Of course. I'm always nervous. But I'm more excited than anything else."

The door of the airplane was lowered, and passengers began to exit. Sharon straightened up, and Shang Ik stood on his toes, straining to see. He pulled his hand up to his chest in a futile attempt to steady his heartbeat. His children noticed the shift in their father's demeanor and came to stand at attention near their parents.

"How will we know her, *Appa*?" asked Sarah, hopping up and down on one foot as if it would give her a better view.

Shang Ik placed his hand on his daughter's head. "Don't worry. You'll know."

The little family waited eagerly, holding on to one another, the children feeding off their father's excitement. Eventually a small woman emerged from the plane, holding in her hands a medium-size bag and a pot with a single pink-hued hibiscus flower, also known as the rose of Sharon.

Shang Ik nudged his wife, Sharon. "See? There's your flower."

She laughed and waved at the woman. The children also began to wave and jump up and down, taking turns shouting. *"Halmeoni! Halmeoni!* Over here!"

The old woman made her way over to where they stood, walking straight to the Korean man surrounded by his Anglo wife and American children. The man reached over the cord that separated them, placing both hands on her cheeks that were already wet with tears.

"Hello, *Eomma.* Welcome home."

The Bulletproof Missionary Book Club Discussion Guide

These questions were created to help generate discussion among your book group. They serve only as a guide. You may not cover each question, or you may add questions of your own depending on the flow of your conversation. The goal is to provoke interesting discussions about the book.

1. Did you like the book? What did you like about it? Dislike?

2. In your opinion, what is the theme or main message of the book?

3. When Shang Ik Moon lived in Seoul, his father made him honor his commitment to attend a Christian church with a classmate. How important was this event?

4. "I am with you always." Shang Ik first heard this phrase attending church with his Christian classmate and later recalled it as he struggled to survive a night in the mountains with his baby cousin. In your opinion, did desperation, hope or something divine cause him to recall these words?

5. Shang Ik survived the danger of living in a war zone, endured the death of family members and faced starvation. How did these tragic events help shape the man he is today? What feelings did his story evoke from you?

6. Many of the atrocities Shang Ik witnessed still exist today – war, poverty, hunger and senseless killings in our

communities. What can one person do to help alleviate the suffering in and outside our country? What can our church communities do?

7. An American fighter pilot killed Shang Ik's sister. An American chaplain, Chaplain Vajda, helped Shang Ik and transformed his life. Discuss Shang Ik's contrasting experiences with Americans in Korea? Do you think he might have had conflicting opinions of Americans or their involvement in Korea?

8. Dr. Shang Ik Moon faced death a number of times as a teenager during the Korean War. Can you recall several instances when his life was threatened? Dr. Moon believes he survived these events because God had a

purpose for him. Have you ever felt that God had a purpose for you?

9. If you had the chance to ask Shang Ik one question, what would it be?

10.   How can we support missionaries, like Dr. Moon, who reach out to new immigrants in our county?

11.   Would you read another book in the series about modern day missionaries?

12.   On scale from 1 - 5, with "5" being the highest, how would you rate this book?

Citations

Bradley, James. *The Imperial Cruise: A Secret History of Empire and War*. New York: Little, Brown, 2009.

Cheevers, Jack. *Act of War: Lyndon Johnson, North Korea, and the Capture of the Spy Ship* Pueblo. New York: NAL Caliber, 2013.

Hearn, Chester G. *Air Force: An Illustrated History: The US Air Force from 1910 to the 21st Century*. Minneapolis: Zenith Press, 2008.

"Korean Family and Kinship Terms." The Talking Cupboard. Accessed January 23, 2018. https://thetalkingcupboard.com/2013/05/11/korean-family-and-kinship-terms.

"Miracle Journey: Rev. Dr. Shang-Ik Moon." Concordia University Irvine. Accessed January 23, 2018. https://www.cui.edu/aboutcui/heritage/fortie th-anniversary/articles/post/miracle-journey.

Made in the USA
Las Vegas, NV
12 December 2020